My Country Has Fallen and It Can't Get Up

What Happened To Accountability?

Judy Forster

Bloomington, IN  Milton Keynes, UK

authorHOUSE™

AuthorHouse™
1663 Liberty Drive, Suite 200
Bloomington, IN 47403
www.authorhouse.com
Phone: 1-800-839-8640

AuthorHouse™ UK Ltd.
500 Avebury Boulevard
Central Milton Keynes, MK9 2BE
www.authorhouse.co.uk
Phone: 08001974150

This book is a work of non-fiction. Unless otherwise noted, the author and the publisher make no explicit guarantees as to the accuracy of the information contained in this book and in some cases, names of people and places have been altered to protect their privacy.

First published by AuthorHouse   4/6/2006

ISBN: 1-4259-2189-2 (sc)

Library of Congress Control Number: 2006902209

Printed in the United States of America
Bloomington, Indiana

This book is printed on acid-free paper.

ACKNOWLEDGEMENTS

This book would not have been possible without the love, and positive encouragement and support from my dear husband, children and friends.

I spent a major part of my life trying to figure out what I was sent here on earth to do. I don't know if it was this book or not, but a force drove me to pull all this together and make available to others.

I don't know if it is a book worth reading, but it was a book worth writing and now it has been done.

You may not agree with all of what is contained, but I think everyone has to agree the following has truth in why we are, where we are, in America today.

If you agree, gather together those with the same feelings and lets join forces to make our voices heard and we can make a difference.

To my wonderful husband, our wonderful children, our terrific grandchildren and our dear friends, I love and thank you all.

HELL YEAH!!!

I like big cars, big boats, big motorcycles, big houses and big campfires.

I believe the money I make, belongs to me and my family, not some governmental stooge with a bad comb-over who wants to give it away to crack addicts for squirting out babies.

Guns do not make you a killer I think killing makes you a killer. You can kill someone with a baseball bat or a car, but no one is trying to ban you from driving to the ball game.

I believe they are called the Boy Scouts for a reason; that is why there are no girls allowed. Girls belong in the Girl Scouts!

I think, that if you feel homosexuality is wrong, it is not a phobia; it is an opinion.

I don't think being a minority makes you a victim of anything except numbers.

The only things I can think of that are truly discriminatory are things like the United Negro College Fund, Jet Magazine, Black Entertainment Television, and Miss Black America.

Try to have things like the United Caucasian College Fund, Cloud Magazine, White Entertainment Television, or Miss White America and see what happens. Jesse Jackson will be knocking down your door.

I have the right "NOT" to be tolerant of others because they are different, weird, or tick me off.

When 70% of the people who get arrested are black, in cities where 70% of the population is black, that is not racial profiling, it is the law of statistics.

I know what sex is, and there are not varying degrees of it. If I received sex from one of my subordinates in my office, it wouldn't be a private matter or my personal business. I would be "FIRED" immediately!

I believe that if you are selling me a milk shake, a pack of cigarettes, a newspaper or a hotel room, you must do it in English! As a matter of fact, if you want to be an American citizen you should have to speak English!

My father and grandfather should not have died in vain so you can leave the countries you were born in to come over and disrespect ours.

I think the police should have every right to shoot your sorry ass if you threaten them after they tell you to stop.

If you can't understand the order "freeze" or "stop" in English, see the above lines.

I feel much safer letting a machine with no political affiliation recount votes when needed. I know what the definition of lying is.

I don't think just because you were not born in this country, you are qualified for any special loan programs, government sponsored bank loans or tax breaks, etc., so you can open a hotel, coffee shop, trinket store, or any other business.

We did not go to the aid of certain foreign countries and risk our lives in wars to defend their freedoms, so that decades later they could come over here and tell us our constitution is a living document and open to their interpretations.

I don't hate the rich. I don't pity the poor.

I know wrestling is fake, but so are movies and television, and that doesn't stop you from watching them.

I believe a self-righteous liberal or conservative with a cause is more dangerous than a Hell's Angel with an attitude.

I think Bill Gates has every right to keep every penny he made and continue to make more. If it ticks you off, go and invent the next operating system that's better and put your name on the building. Ask your buddy (Al Gore) that invented the Internet to help you…

It doesn't take a whole village to raise a child right, but it does take a parent to stand up to the kid and smack his/her little ass when necessary and say "NO".

I think tattoos and piercing are fine if you want them, but please don't pretend they are a political statement. And please stay home until that new lip ring heals, I don't want to look at your ugly infected mouth as you serve me French fries!

I am sick of "Political Correctness" and of all the suck ups that go along with it. I know a lot of black people, and not a single one of them was born in Africa, so how can they be "African Americans"? Besides, Africa is a continent. I don't go around saying I am a European-American because my great, great, great, great, great, great grandfather was from Europe. I am proud to be from America and no where else.

And if you don't like my point of view, tough! GET OVER IT!!! WAKE UP WHILE YOU STILL HAVE A COUNTRY TO WAKE UP TO. (Author Unknown).

This totally sums up how I feel, and you know what? I am finding that I am not alone!!!

CHAPTER 1
WHERE DID THIS TITLE COME FROM?

I never thought of myself as a racist, in fact, I tried very hard not to become one, but there are some who will think this book is, which I guess will include me.

The events since Hurricane Katrina have served as unbelievable revelations to my husband & me, and obviously to many other friends, family members and even total strangers.

We became angry, and not just the type of anger that would pass over night.

The visuals on television made it worse. Not that we believe everything we see and hear, we have been around too long to fall for that, but we do believe there are still a few unbiased newscasters, and those are the ones we listen to.

At my age, I guess I have waited for someone else to do something about the current state of things in our great country, the country my father fought to keep free in World War II, the country my husband fought for, as our country tried to help the plight of those during Viet Nam, and the country that my son volunteered to serve and went off to fight during the Gulf War, on the DMZ and in Bosnia. We are just one family who proudly contains many valiant protectors of peace and freedom. I am blessed, all three of my heroes, whom, I know and love, came home alive.

I see and hear those who want us to cut and run - Kennedy, Murtha, Pelosi, Boxer, and Reid. You know who they are. We are trying, not only to keep this horrible sneaky new enemy from our shores again; but also to show those they have used and abused, that they too can have peace and freedom. We are showing them the way to freedom. This is a noble and a responsible thing to do.

So where do these people, who would not have the right to say the stupid things they say, if it was not for all of those who died before, giving us freedom, come from? I wish I knew. Just being a democrat and taking the opposing view does not make sense. They are not held accountable for any of the garbage they throw out there and just walk away from. We need to hold all government officials' feet to the fire for all they say, do and promote. They had better have their ducks in a row or "strike three" and you are out, and out for good! We put them at that post, and by golly, we can remove them.

I see people hanging around, doing nothing all day, (many of which could be in a service uniform helping their fellow citizens fight the good fight instead of partying at night or taking things that are not theirs, things and lives.

I see children growing up in filth and shabbiness, around people who will not work, who blame others for their blight, people who find it easier to take what belongs to someone else, rather than work for it.

I see foreigners coming into our country some legally, but so many not. No one seems to care. We have changed our lives to fit theirs. Is that not incredible? They don't, nor do they want to learn our language, they demand that we add a second language or more to make their lives easier.

Sorry, they came here, we didn't go get them and bring them here by force.

Paul Harvey says: I don't believe in Santa Claus, but I'm not going to sue somebody for singing a Ho-Ho-Ho song in December. I don't agree with Darwin, but I didn't go out and hire a lawyer when my high school teacher taught his theory of evolution.

Life, liberty or your pursuit of happiness will not be endangered because someone says a 30-second prayer before a football game.

So what's the big deal? It's not like somebody is up there reading the entire book of Acts. They're just talking to a God they believe in and asking him to grant safety to the players on the field and the fans going home from the game.

"But it's a Christian prayer," some will argue. Yes, and this is the United States of America, a country founded on Christian principles. According to our very own phone book, Christian churches outnumber all others better than 200-to-1. So what would you expect-somebody chanting Hare Krishna?

If I went to a football game in Jerusalem, I would expect to hear a Jewish prayer.

If I went to a soccer game in Baghdad, I would expect to hear a Muslim prayer.

If I went to a ping-pong match in China, I would expect to hear someone pray to Buddha. And I wouldn't be offended. It wouldn't bother me one bit.

When in Rome ..

"But what about the atheists?" What about them?

Nobody is asking them to be baptized. We're not going to pass the collection plate.

Just humor us for 30 seconds. If that's asking too much, bring a Walkman or a pair of earplugs. Go to the bathroom. Visit the concession stand. Call your lawyer!

Unfortunately, one or two will make that call. One or two will tell thousands what they can and cannot do I don't think a short prayer at a football game is going to shake the world's foundations.

Christians are just sick and tired of turning the other cheek while our courts strip us of all our rights. Our parents and grandparents taught us to pray before eating; to pray before we go to sleep.

Our Bible tells us to pray without ceasing. Now a handful of people and their lawyers are telling us to cease praying.

God, help us. And if that last sentence offends you, well ... just sue me.

The silent majority has been silent too long. It's time we let that one or two who scream loud enough to be heard .... that the vast majority don't care what they want. It is time the majority rules! It's time we tell them, you don't have to pray; you don't have to say the pledge of allegiance; you don't have to believe in God or attend services that honor Him. That is your right, and we will honor your right. But by golly, you are no longer going to take our rights away. We are fighting back ... and we WILL WIN!

God bless us one and all ... especially those who denounce Him. God bless America, despite all her faults. She is still the greatest nation of all.

God bless our service men, who, are fighting to protect our right to pray and worship God.

May 2005, be the year the silent majority is heard and we put God back as the foundation of our families and institutions.

Keep looking up.

I feel that our country has fallen because criminals have more rights than victims (Criminal Justice system). We have to search a community before buying a home to see how many sex offenders live there, so we can avoid it. We have to spend extra money for security systems on our homes, cars and anything else we can arm with one. You can not trust a priest with your child, you can not trust a pretty teacher at your child's school, you can not trust the person sitting next to you on a plane. You have to buy a shredder to shred everything in your garbage so someone cannot steal your identity. WHY?

People will tell you it is a sign of the times, I say it is because we have allowed ourselves to become prey to people who won't work to get the money needed to buy things they want, or people who find it easier to escape a perfectly good life by living on drugs and alcohol and can not hold a job, and blame everyone but themselves for their problems. People are allowed to walk out of court after raping a small child over and over because a Vermont Judge (whom we allowed to be placed on the bench) no longer believes in punishment??? The Judge and the child molester should be sent to Alaska to exist naked in a 6' by 6' stainless steel cell with nothing but bread and water for the rest of their natural life. Harsh, no I don't think so. What about the poor child? Someone who will be tormented for the rest of their natural life for what happened to them. The child did not ask for what happened to them, in many cases they are made to feel like it was their fault. Why? Because some depraved idiot cannot control their urges? That some idiot Judge has forgotten the reason they studied law and were ultimately given the privilege to serve on the Bench. No more! Remember, "Thou shalt not kill, though shalt not steal, just to name 2!

Many will say our world is so screwed up because so many are poverty stricken. Let me give you some facts about poverty. From a Census Data report by Robert E. Rector & Kirk A. Johnson, PhD "Backgrounder #1713".

Poverty is an important and emotional issue and the recent Census Bureau info declared that there were nearly 35 million poor persons in the country in 2002, only a small increase from 2001.

They said to understand this word poverty, we need to look at the actual living conditions of the individuals the government deems to be poor. Please note the words government deems to be poor.

In its pure form, the word "poverty" suggests destitution and inability to provide a family with nutritious food, clothing, and reasonable shelter. Only a small number of the 35 million classified as "poor", by the Census Bureau, fit that description. Most of America's poor live in, material conditions that would be judged as comfortable or well off just a few generations ago. Today the expenditures per person of the lowest-income of one-fifth of households equal those of the median American household in the early 1970s after adjusting for inflation.

The following facts come from several government reports.

1. 46% of all poor households actually own their own homes. The average home owned by persons classified as poor by the Census Bureau is a 3-bedroom house with 1 ½ baths, a garage and a porch or patio.

2. 76% of poor households have air conditioning. By contrast 30 years ago only 36% enjoyed air conditioning.

3. Only 6% are overcrowded – more than 2/3s have more than 2 rooms per person.

4. The average poor American has more living space than the average individual living in Paris, London, Vienna, Athens, and other cities throughout Europe, and these are compared to average citizens in these foreign countries, not poor.

5. Nearly 3/4s of poor households own a car, 30% own 2 or more.

6.   97% of poor households have a color TV, over half own 2 or more color TVs.

7.   78% have a VCR or DVD player, 62% have cable or satellite TV reception.

8.   73% own microwave ovens, more than half have a stereo, and a third have an automatic dishwasher.

9.   As a group, America's poor are far from being chronically undernourished. The average consumption of protein, vitamins, and minerals is virtually the same for poor and middle class children and in most cases is well above recommended norms. Poor children actually consume more meat than do high income-children and have average protein intakes 100 percent above recommended levels.

Most poor children today are, in fact, super-nourished and grow up to be on average inch taller and 10 pounds heavier than that of the GIs who stormed the beaches of Normandy in World War II.

The poor are generally well nourished, 89% reported they have enough food to eat and only 2% said they did not.

Overall, the typical American defined as poor by the government has a car, air conditioning, a refrigerator, at stove, a washer and dryer and a microwave. He/she has 2 color TVS, cable or satellite TV reception, a VCR or DVD player and a stereo. He/she is also able to obtain medical care. His home is in good repair and in not overcrowded. By his own report, his family is not hungry and he had sufficient funds in the past year to meet his family essential needs.

While not opulent in some cases, it is equally far from the popular images of dire poverty conveyed by the press, liberal activist and politicians.

Over a ¼ of poor households had cell phones and telephone answering machines.

Roughly a third do experience at least one problem such as overcrowding, temporary hunger or difficulty getting medical care.

Sorry, Jesse, Al & Charlie! What you guys like to throw out about the poor is not quite correct.

They went on to report that, there were two main reasons that American children are poor.

Their parents don't work much and fathers are absent from the home. Oh really!!!!! Just ride around some of your so called poor neighborhoods any given day and any given hour, you will see people very capable of working, just standing or sitting around.

In good economic times or bad, the typical poor family with children is supported by only 800 hours of work during a year. That amounts to 16 hours of work per week. If work in each family were raised to 2000 hours per year, the equivalent of one adult working 40 hours per week throughout the year, nearly 75% of poor children would be lifted out of the official poverty category.

Nearly 2/3s of poor children reside in single parent homes, each year an additional 1.3 million children are born out of wedlock. If poor mothers married the fathers of their children, almost 3/4s would immediately be lifted out of poverty.

If poverty means lacking nutritious food, adequate warm housing and clothing for a family, relatively few of the 35 million people identified as being in poverty would be characterized as poor.

It has been found that when the Temporary Assistance to Needy Families TANF (1996), which replaced the old Aid to Families with Dependent Children required that some welfare mothers either prepare for work or get jobs as a condition of receiving aid, welfare rolls plummeted and employment of single mothers increased in an unprecedented manner. As employment of single mothers rose, child poverty dropped rapidly.

Even in the TANF program, over half the adult beneficiaries are idle on the rolls of assistance and are not engaged in activities leading to self-sufficiency. Work requirements are virtually non-existent in related programs, such as food stamps, and public housing. The welfare system continues to encourage idle dependence, rather than work and to reward single parenthood while penalizing marriage.

In conclusion to this report, it was found that the living conditions of persons defined as poor by the government bear little resemblance to notions of poverty held by the general public.

By increasing work and marriage, our nations can virtually eliminate remaining child poverty.

Robert E. Rector is Senior Research Fellow in Domestic Policy Studies and Kirk A. Johnson, PHD is a Harry and Jeannette Weinberg Fellow in Statistical Welfare Research in the Center for Data Analysis at The Heritage Foundation.

We lived many years in Washington, DC. It got to the point that when I went to Wal-mart, I was the "minority". Yes white, American, spoke English and dressed in normal all American clothes.

I was surrounded with people who could hardly speak English, who dressed in anything from a Sari to some sort of wrap around their head, by cashiers who stared at me blankly when the cash register would not work, because they were banging on it, instead of reading the English instructions on the screen telling them what to do. Obviously, unable to understand the English! She did not even understand when I asked her to call a Supervisor for help. Finally, out of frustration, I reached past her and pushed the correct button so my check would go through the device. Maddening, you bet!

Living in the nation's capital I saw first hand how the game is played. I would like to believe that most of those we elect to represent us, our hopes and dreams, do go to their new job as "public servant" with the best intentions. I know not all of them do, but I will believe that most do, at first, take their responsibility seriously. Briefly, it seems. I love those words Public Servants. So far from what they actually end up being.

They immediately get caught up in the "game" of politics and the intentions they had, now can be swayed by votes, money and power. How very sad! To all of them I say, Thank you for forgetting why you were sent there in the first place – to represent those who gave you the job! Thank you for forgetting all of those promises you made to us to make change for us, to protect us, to voice our needs. I will tell you one thing you have not had any problem doing, and that is spending our tax dollars with no regard for how we want it spent. You spend and spend and never any accountability for how! You will lie, cheat, and expect to go back for another term to do it again. Your days are numbered!

We have been given away, we have been sold and now we have fallen, and I am not sure we can get up. I do know this family is not going to give up though, you can call it conservative, you can call it right wing, whatever, but we believe in truth, honesty, hard work, and equal rights for those willing to do the right thing.

You see, I think, and this is my opinion, that if you are going to dole out my money, and you dole it out in reckless abandon, you don't get a second chance.

Your job is at our discretion, not just a God given right once you warm you chair.

When I watch the likes of Byrd, and Kennedy, just to name a few, decade after decade, reporting for duty, I cringe. Year after year, election after election, they are just fat and happy and laughing all the way to the bank. They are enjoying the many benefits they get, taking their big paychecks, built on all of those pay increases they vote for themselves at 3 a.m., the retirement for them and their spouses, that they don't contribute to, and you goofy people in their states, just keep letting them go back. What are you getting for your dollar? Not much that I can see. Kennedy just slings stuff out there and turns and walks away, no accountability, no basis, no reason in many cases, he just can, and you let him and the rest like him.

Poor Sen. Byrd needs to hang on to the podium anytime he begins his orations, pointing a finger at so many others, so many times without fact or support, this former KKK member should not be casting any stones and should be back home in West Virginia enjoying what days he has left. I ask his constituents, what are you getting out of this man, what kind of job is he doing?

They seem to have a "free pass" to just show up, rant and rave, and turn and walk away. I don't see our dollars worth for their being put back in office time and time again to do the same thing, year after year, and of course no accountability for their actions. Name one thing any of them have done that was for the good of you or me in the last 10 years??? I would say they did not meet or fully satisfy the job requirements they were sent to meet. Not even "fully successful", if you ask me.

President Clinton even went so far as to have his sexual fantasies come to life in the house we let him live in. We even gave him camera time to protest his innocence, then, beg for forgiveness once he was cornered. There are even those who seem to have bought the bill of goods that he was not impeached. Excuse me, he was impeached, he was just not removed from office. Impeached is impeached, just like being pregnant.

These so called Public Servants should have to show us what they have done, they need to give us their timesheets, they need to have to save up their sick leave and vacation time and use it like the rest of us. They need to put money into their retirement accounts and pay into social security like we do. No wonder they have no real sense of urgency for solving that issue, it does not impact them! No more free vacations on our dimes, especially in the name of doing political work.

Trust me, if they did have to give us an outline of what they promised, what they actually achieved, and we know how many days they were on the job, how many votes did they make, just what have they done to deserve our returning them to their position. You might actually see some real work out of them.

When John Kerry ran for President, there was some research done into his voting record, and the survey said – it was abysmal! His failure to even show up to vote – a very big part of his job, is just the tip of the iceberg. Even when he did vote, he was all over the map. It appears it just depended on "what was in it for him".

He is not alone. No free vacations with the disguise of doing something for you or me. We don't get vacations like that, why should they – remember the words – PUBLIC SERVANT! No raise unless they did a good job and WE THE PEOPLE approve it. We want progress reports. We will grade them, we will decide if they move to the next grade. I don't want to hear that progress report from them either, I want these things published by someone unbiased and we should not have to pay for the service or have to go searching the Internet for the information. Just more examples of how things have gotten out of hand. It is next to impossible to find out this info unless you are some computer guru or attend all of the congressional sessions to count heads and listen to the votes.

I believe, that all members of Congress should be under the same guidelines as a President, Two terms max. At least the special interest groups are going to realllllllyyyyy have to work for it, to only have 4 or 12 years to get them in their back pockets. Then they would have to start all over again with new people.

Ya know, they (the special interest clan) might just decide it was not cost affective.

This term idea would pass, if we all ban together and demand it. It should be on the ballot for the 2008 election.

Crazy things find their way into Bills on the Hill. One of them is that we should pay Reparations to those whose ancestors were sold as slaves. The next time I hear that we should pay reparations for what happened way back before my Dad was a twinkle in his Dad's eye, I am going to send the following to the person throwing out such garbage.

Slavery Reparations by Fred Reed

On the Web I find that Henry Louis Gates Jr., the chairman of Afro- American Studies at Harvard, is demanding that whites pay reparations to blacks. See, it's because of slavery.

He is joined in this endeavor by a gaggle of other professional blacks. I guess he'll send me a bill, huh?

I feel like saying, "Let me get this straight, Hank. I'm slow. Be patient. You want free money because of slavery, right? I don't blame you." I'd like free money too. Tell you what. I believe in justice. I'll give you a million dollars for every slave I own, and another million for every year you were a slave. Fair enough?

But tell me, how many slaves do you suppose I have? In round numbers, I mean. Say to the nearest dozen. And how long were you a slave?

Oh. In other words, I owe you reparations for something that I didn't do and didn't happen to you. That makes sense. Like lug nuts on a birthday cake.

Personally, I think you owe me reparations for things you didn't do and never happened to me. I've never been coated in Dutch chocolate and thrown from the Eiffel Tower. I'll bet you've never done it to anyone. I want reparations.

Kinda silly, isn't it?

But if we're going to talk about reparations, that's a street that runs in two directions. You want money from me for what some other whites did to some other blacks in another century. How about you guys paying whites reparations for current expenses caused by blacks?

Not long ago blacks burned down half of Los Angeles, a city in my country. Cities are expensive, Hank. Build one sometime and you'll see what I mean.

Whites had to pay taxes to repair Los Angeles for you. You can send me a check. Now, yes, I know you burned LA because you didn't like the verdict in the trial of those police officers. Well, I didn't like the verdict in the Simpson trial. But I didn't burn my house and loot Korean grocers.

Over the years blacks have burned a lot of American cities: Newark, Detroit, Watts, on and on.

Now add in the fantastic cost over the years of welfare in all its forms, of large police forces and jails and security systems in department stores.

I can't live in the capital city of my own country because of crime committed by blacks. Toss in the cultural cost of lowering standards in everything for the benefit of blacks. See what I mean?

Now, I'd view things differently if you said, "Fred, blacks can't get anywhere in a modern country without education. We know that.

We need better schools, smarter teachers, harder courses, books with smaller pictures and bigger words. Can you help us?"

I'd say, "Hallelujah! Hoo-ahh! Not just yes, but hell yes. Let's sell an aircraft carrier and get these folks some real schools and get them into the economic mainstream" I'd say it partly because it would be the right thing to do, and partly, because I'd like to add you guys to the tax base.

The current custodial state is expensive. I'd just love for blacks to study and learn to compete and stop burning places. But is it going to happen?

You may not believe it, but I, and most whites, don't like seeing blacks as miserable and screwed up as they are. I spend a fair amount of time in the projects. Those places are ugly. It's no fun watching perfectly good kids turn into semiliterate dope dealers who barely speak English. It just plain ain't right.

But, Hank, what am I supposed to do about it? I can't do your children's homework.. At some point, people have to do things for themselves, or they don't get done. Maybe it's time.

I'll tell you what I see out in the world, Hank.. I think blacks are too accustomed to getting anything they want by just demanding it.

True, it has worked for over half a century. Get a few hundred people in the street, implicitly threaten to loot and burn, holler about slavery, and the Great Whit e Cash Spigot turns on. Thing is, whites don't much buy it any longer. Most recognize that what once was a civil- rights movement has become a shakedown game. Few people still feel responsible for the failings and inadequacies of blacks. Political correctness keeps the lid on – but everyone knows the score.

Which scares me, Hank.

On one hand, blacks hate whites and incline toward looting and burning. (The whites you hate are the ones who marched in the civil-rights movement. Ever think about that?)

On the other hand, whites quietly grow wearier and wearier of it. Not good.

On the third hand (allow me three hands, for rhetorical convenience), blacks keep demanding things. As I write, you demand reparations for slavery.

Blacks in Oklahoma (I think it was) want money for some ancient race riot. Other blacks reject the Declaration of Independence, blacks in New York hint broadly at burning and looting over a trial, yet more demand the elimination of the Confederate flag, and the federal equal opportunity apparatus, which means blacks, want to sue Silicon Valley for not hiring nonexistent black engineers.

That's a lot of demanding for one month, Hank. What happens if whites ever say, "No"? How, how about you?

You've got a cushy job up there at Harvard, and you can hoot and holler about what swine and bandits whites are. I guess it's lots of fun, and you get a salary for it. But don't you think you might do blacks more good if you told them to complain less and study more?

For example, if you want blacks to work in Silicon Gulch, the best approach might be to find some really smart black guys, and get them to study digital design, not Black Studies. That's how everybody else does it. It works. Then blacks wouldn't feel left out, and racial tension would decline.

Sound like a plan?

Just out of curiosity, how many hours a week, do professors of Afro-American Studies spend in the projects, encouraging poor black kids to study real life sho-nuf subjects?

Fred

CHAPTER 2
HURRICANE KATRINA AND THE EMAILS

THE POSTMAN'S CORNER

In 1927, a major unnamed hurricane struck the city of New Orleans. It was actually more powerful than Katrina. The scope of damage was much more severe because this particular hurricane actually hit the city, Katrina missed it by 25 miles.

The interesting difference is the response the government gave in 1927 to those hurricane refugees, compared to the refugees of Katrina, err – I mean "survivors" – sorry Al Sharpton and Jesse Jackson.

How much aid did the government dispense at that time? Zero, nada, not one dime.

And you know how much aid the army offered? The only aid from the army came in the form of loaning the city of New Orleans tents and camp stoves. Ironically, later the army sued the city for reimbursement. So what was the big difference here?

It was the attitude the people had towards the government at that time, compared to the attitude that Katrina's victims have. The 1927 "survivors" expected nothing from the government. Eighty year ago, people understood that the government was there to "protect life, liberty and the pursuit of happiness." That's a major difference. And now, a week later, when the government failed on all three levels of local, state, and federal to provide for their needs, Americans were sorely disappointed.

Reverends Jackson and Sharpton spend their opportunities arguing about semantics. "They shouldn't be called refugees, they should be called survivors".

Unfortunately, they missed the boat. It was a perfect opportunity to deliver a very basic message to their people.

Fact, if you are poor and uneducated in American, this is what happens.

Fact, if you depend on the government, you will be sorely disappointed.

Fact, if you are poor in America, there is no reason for you to be uneducated. It's free! 12 grades. And if you really apply yourself, there is enough grants and assistance out there for higher education, which will raise you above the poverty level. And no longer will you depend on the government and be disappointed. It's unfortunate that this lesson will be missed by most of the "survivors".

A couple of other points should be brought to light. G. W. has asked the congress for 50 billion dollars worth of aid for the survivors and clean up of the city. Interesting isn't it one million people displaced and out of work in that city, sitting all day in shelters waiting for the next handout. Of course, the thought never occurred to anyone that just maybe, hey, we should give all of these folks, jobs filling sand bags to plug the levees and clearing trees. I wonder how many them would want government aid if they had to work for it?

And finally, they have hardly begun the task of picking up dead bodies and already the finger pointed has started. The congressional hearings and probes will go forever. Millions will be spent on a wasted diatribe of a bipartisan "witch hunting expedition" - all of which will be nonsense. If you're a democrat, you are going to blame the President. If you are republican, you are going to blame the mayor and the governor. This is another case in point of how the government will once again fail its people, they could have spent the millions educating the poor and misplaced citizens of New Orleans so that they could go out and get a new and better life, instead of wasting it on useless blame investigations.

Well, I'm just a dumb redneck joke teller and certainly not educated enough to run my government. I'm sure that there are plenty of people out there who will tell me why my ideas and thoughts will not work. Maybe I should just stick to joke telling, eh?

Signed, Martin aka The Postman, Editor "The Postman's Corner"

This was another email we received and it had been passed around to great numbers.

A resident of McComb, MS. (a town about 80 miles north of New Orleans) said he saw the poor and the wealthy, of all skin colors, hurt by the storm, he saw Christian people giving, giving, giving. He saw Churches going all out to minister in Jesus' name, Neighbors going, door to door helping one another. Thugs and hoodlums going, door to door, looking for someone vulnerable. He saw ice and water being fought over as police tried to keep the peach. He saw people coming up from New Orleans taking over empty houses because shelters are full. He saw out of town volunteers coming with food and staying for however long it took to serve it. He saw the Red Cross, the Salvation Army doing a great job, however they could. He saw Four hundred crewmen from everywhere bring back the power to the homes, churches and businesses. He saw mile long gas lines. He saw the National Guardsmen patrolling the streets of McComb, along with the Kentucky policemen protecting the McComb inhabitants, from the hoodlums and thugs of McComb, Pike County and New Orleans. He saw drug dealers still working outside the shelters. He saw doctors, nurses and other hospital personnel working tirelessly even sleeping in the hospital to do the job God called them to do.

What no one saw, including the McComb resident, the ACLU, people from the American Way, NAACP, American Atheist organization or Jesse, Al or Louis helping, serving, writing big checks, handing out debit cards or anything else for that matter.

No they were very, very busy, agitating and stirring the race cards in their pots! Silly me, what did I expect?

We must have all missed seeing Hillary, Chuck, Teddy & Kerry, maybe even Mama "T", standing there sweating with the volunteers and handing out food, water, ice or directing gas station traffic? I know I did.

There were whole communities who never saw a camera crew or anyone else for weeks, but guess what? They did not sit and cry, "What are you going to give me or do for me"! No, they grabbed what they could salvage, which, in most cases was not much; they found heavy equipment and started moving the debris to make way for recovery.

Some hoisted make shift tents, and stayed to protect what little they had left. They helped their neighbors, their friends and neighbors pulled together to feed, clothe and clean up! What an amazing saga. They did not wait for help to come to them, they did not wait for someone to spend millions of dollars to save them, to take them to a nice clean place where nice people would cook for them, clean up for them, take them wherever they wanted to go and at no cost to them.

After Katrina –NEW ORLEANS, Nov. 16, 2005

New Orleans police say they have never seen so much peace and quiet on the city's streets. We haven't seen a robbery since the beginning of August," said Lt. Troy Savage, who patrols what was once the city's most violent neighborhood. "We're probably at this point, one of the safest communities in the United States," he said.

Police said a woman was stabbed to death Tuesday night the first such incident in 90 days, a record in this city.

Since Hurricane Katrina forced most of the residents to relocate, police say, the daily shootings and killings have stopped.

"This was the most lethal criminal underclass in the United States," said Dr. Peter Scharf, director of the University of New Orleans Center for Society, Law and Justice. "We were heading for a murder rate of 72 per 100,000. New York City is at seven."

Scharf says, according to city records, there were 265 murders in New Orleans last year, 258 murders in 2003, and 275 in 2002.

Warren J. Riley, New Orleans' acting superintendent of police, says the drug dealers and gangs evacuated with the residents and haven't returned.

"We're a small town; we're Mayberry right now," Riley said.

Crime Wave Spreads …

By some estimates, hardcore criminals in New Orleans numbered in the tens of thousands, and they're now living in other cities Baton Rouge, Dallas, Atlanta, and Houston.

Houston Police Chief Harold Hurtt says crime is up in neighborhoods where large numbers of evacuees have settled.

He says he needs 400 new officers and has asked the Federal Emergency Management Agency for financial assistance.

"We're not going to let anyone come into the city and break the law at will," Hurtt said. Last week, Houston police arrested a New Orleans man charged with four murders.

In Georgia, police have been busy busting alleged New Orleans drug dealers trying set up shop in and around Atlanta.

As a result, residents in some places are beginning to roll up the welcome mat. It's a criminal element some cities didn't expect, and New Orleans doesn't want back.

Well, I guess New Orleans will not have to put more non-existent police officers back on their payroll now. That's right, it seems they had a phantom police roster, so the story goes, if they put out there that they had so many police officers, crime would be deterred. Guess what, it did not work. Oh Yes, and where did all the money go that was being allocated to these non-existent police officers pay and their benefits?? There could be a real good reason the New Orleans Police Chief did not want to be Chief anymore?? Could the truth be coming out?? Mayor Nagin, any comment??? Gov. Blanco, you must have something to say about this??? Silence...... Who is going to be held accountable?

Imagine That!

There it was! The Reality! I say to you, my fellow Americans, – those of you who work hard, pay taxes as designated by your government, evacuate when someone of authority tells you too, gives it there level best to raise their children themselves, care for their homes, cars and respect other people's property — get out your checkbooks folks, and order more checks, it is going to be a bumpy ride to pay for those who choose to take the lazy, easy way out.

Over the 50 plus years of my life, I have witnessed scandals, crime and the like right within the halls of our government buildings. It has only worsened by the day it seems. There is so much finger pointing, setting other officials up any way they can, they should all be in "time out"!

I think that if you are going to point a finger, you had better be sure you are "lily white yourself" and you had better have concrete proof to offer up to back your insinuation. If not, I don't want my tax dollars wasted on one more investigation or grand jury just for your witch hunts. If you have lied, made something up or planted something to make someone else look bad, then you are in bigger trouble, and you will not be respected you will not skate, you will be prosecuted.

I was always taught, you have to do the right thing and you will be rewarded for it. I tried to raise my son that way, and with the good Lord's help, was successful.

You are accountable for your actions, is still echoing in my head from when I was a child, and my parents preached that point endlessly, I guess I became my Mother in some ways, because I said the same to my son and now to my grandchildren.

I also was taught that there are no free rides. You work hard, you don't steal, you don't lie, you keep your nose to the grindstone, you go to church, do the right thing, even when no one is watching.

My goodness, those are not rocket science things to believe and live are they? Well, we have managed to allow our Country's decision makers – those we elected into power, to give our tax dollars away to everyone in the world, and spend them on the most ridiculous things with out anyone saying – No!

We have allowed them to make decisions, implement those decisions, only to have the next regime come in and reverse it all. I cannot even put into numbers the waste that has come from these things being done over and over again. The Iraq war is a penny compared to the waste that our so-called public servants have perpetuated over the last decades. They have banished programs that did not benefit them and their cronies, then the next party comes in and re-institute those same banished programs, one being when the Clinton administration reduced armed services drastically, and additionally reduced civil service. Now I ask you, when 911 occurred, we had to jump to it to get people and weaponry up to power. I heard Congressional leaders on the Democratic side, crying about the money, then they cried about the lack of equipment for our service people. Well, I ask you now, if we had been proactive and kept our armed services at peak, in manpower, and equipment, we would have a few more of them amongst us today, and we would not have had to wait so long before we could strike back.

The cost has been astronomical, and if we would have just done the sensible thing all along, that money could be used for rebuilding after the war. If any of the decision makers are going to put forth their agenda in getting rid of anything, we need to let them know that we want a cost benefit analysis that we get to vote on first. Then we are all on the same page, and if it was the wrong decision, then we are all accountable.

We have witnessed stupid things like, rain forest studies in Iowa and the sexual habits of shrimp, tied to budget approval so the government could continue to run. What a horrible expense and waste of your and my money.

My husband and I worked for the government; we have seen these things happen up close and personal. It is laughable in many instances. As long as we allow some of these yahoos in office it will only continue. We can stop it, but, here is the clincher, it will take most all of us to change it.

Unless we ban together, and we mandate accountability for their decisions, and really hold their feet to the fire, nothing will change. Of course the far left liberals will kick and scream, because they like to call the shots, but there are more of us than them. We, being the God loving, God fearing, honest, hardworking moderates, can turn it around for our children and grandchildren. I may be crazy, but I think we could do this.

CHAPTER 3

ENTITLEMENTS – MY ASS - OR HOW THE LIKES OF JESSE JACKSON, AL SHARPTON, CHARLIE RANGEL- MADE IT POSSIBLE FOR THE POOR TO GROW IN NUMBERS

I was not responsible for the poor being poor, or slavery, nor were my grandparents or there grandparents.

Black people sold black people for slaves! Did you know that? It is true! So I take great offense when the likes of Jesse Jackson, or Al Sharpton, or Charlie Rangel or the great Louis Farrakhan try to lay that one on us.

My family got to where they are by hard work, not looking for anyone to put food or money before us, when we were coming up short. If we were going through hard times, we worked a second job.

I hear the word "entitlements", and I get nuts.

None of us are really entitled to anything, except the air we breathe, the freedoms granted by our Constitution and all that our fellow Americans have fought for and are still fighting for with their lives. I thank them all and the families they left behind. Other than those things, I cannot think of any thing else that we should EXPECT from our fellow citizens via the taxes we all pay.

That word – Entitlements - a word, according to the Webster's Dictionary means – "To furnish with a right"! This is not even a sensible word to use for these so-called programs, but I will tell you one thing, it has cost us unbelievably.

The amount is never enough. From one election to the next, who tells us???? Those wanting the "poor people's' vote, that they need more.

I can drive down some areas of our little southern town only to see shack after shack littered with trash in the front yard, cars with fancy chromed wheels, sitting anywhere there is room, and a line of chairs on the front porch of every one. On any given day, each one of those chairs is holding what certainly seems to be able-bodied so called poor person. They are just sitting there shooting the breeze, waiting for what – probably the next Entitlement offering from you and me, I guess.

This scene is duplicated in city after city, state after state. You have seen it, I know.

They are just hanging out on street corners, driving in their "rides", blaring their thumping rap crap, figuring out where they can put another tattoo or piercing and really, just having a good 'ole' time on your and my dime.

I resent this enormously, but it is not their fault! Yes, you hear it right, not their fault.

Who gave them the right — not to work, not to save, not to payoff anything, not to educate themselves, not to curb their procreation ethics, to feel that to take a life, or anything they want that does not belong to them???

Our elected officials, that's who!

Yep, the ones you sent to Washington, or to your state capital.

Yes, these are the ones who feel, or who were made to feel and try to make us feel, that we owe these folks for something we did not do. Of course it had nothing to do with the votes they would get to return them to their cushy lifestyle in Washington. The special tingle they got every time they pushed through another "gulp" – Entitlement program.

They then pass it on to us and tell us what we have a responsibility to do, and thus, we have taught and continue to teach them how to hold their hands out.

I think the new slaves and the soon to be new poor, are the rest of us whose money is spent for votes by those we put in office! We work, we save, we write the big check to the IRS, to this group and that group, only to have someone take it and give it to people who have been rendered unable to be a contributing citizen.

The poor, to a large degree, is being taught, to just sit back and we will give and give and give, etc., etc., etc., and oh by the way, next year we will do better because your numbers are growing!

Thank you government officials for squandering our money on this monster called "entitlements"! This does not even make sense and has only made the poor, who they are—POOR and we are soon to follow.

These programs that our good government officials have fallen prey too, grow bigger every day. Just ask Charlie Rangel, who stated recently, that, "this President is nothing more than a Bull Connor, and has done nothing to help".

Mr. Rangel, in my humble opinion you must think I am an idiot to believe that!

Even after Bill O'Reilly of the Fox News, "No Spin Zone", held up the numbers proving that President Bush had allocated more than President Clinton ever did, Rangel would still not back down.

This is just another instance of a liberal throwing out something and not being accountable for his words, or his actions and stirring up people, then simply walking away. It never ends!

What we should be doing is tell people, you must do what it takes to be a citizen of this once GREAT COUNTRY. There are no more so called Entitlement programs, no free money, no free food, no free or subsidized housing, no free medical, no free anything. You have to carry your share and do it the old fashioned way – Get educated, Get a job, and earn it!

I can see helping the aged who have nothing, or the children, but the dead-beat dads and moms, no excuses, no way. I did not force you to make the children that you seem to have forgotten you have a responsibility for, either.

If we are going to offer subsidy programs, they have to be monitored, and there is a period certain that it ends, unless otherwise justified, and those perimeters are definite, and put in language you and I and anyone else can understand, and signed off by the person trying to use them. No fudging! No extensions!

No child left behind! That program holds hope. Here is the deal though. Use it to teach kids not to talk like they have a mouth full of mush and use proper English, wear clothes that fit and are clean, walk tall because they are on their way to becoming "somebody", and get any and all education that is at their disposal, no shirking, no excuses.

If you don't attend school and work to get a decent grade – no more money. Go get a job cleaning streets, or digging ditches, where you are doing something to earn your keep, but that will be as good as it gets.

All educators should have the right to discipline. I respected and feared every teacher I had, and that was not a bad thing. I worked as hard as I could for them and; most of all, I knew my parents would not understand anything other than my doing my best. I was always told, "if you get in trouble in school, you will get it double when you get home."

The teachers should not be living in fear of these kids! The teachers should be respected, and yes even feared because they are in power and they rule in their classroom domain. They get paid to educate, they have studied to educate, — Let them do it!

Employers have a responsibility too. Even people working at McDonalds should be compelled to speak clearly and distinctly, move quickly and respect the person who is giving their employer MONEY for services rendered so that they ultimately have a job and get paid themselves. I am tired of being looked at like I just landed from outer space, just because I want fast food at a fast food restaurant!

We all have choices and there are many who came from disadvantaged families and who have made their way to success. It was not just an accident, they care about themselves and their families, but most of all they are doing what it takes to be a responsible American citizen.

You know what they say, you are what you eat! I think you are what you live in, too. Well, it is amazing, that people can allow their children to be raised where there is trash growing in their yards, that their house, is falling down around their porch chair, and why? Probably because they are lazy, and probably because they know we will fix it when we get tired of looking at it. We always do. No accountability folks! You have a responsibility to these kids if you are going to pop them out!

It is easy to see why the rest of the pattern has fallen in place if you have this for an environment and are surrounded with elders who are absolutely no good example, you are what you live in and among.

I have a real problem understanding where the people, like Rev. Jackson get off laying guilt on the rest of the world for all of the poor. Please note – the likes of Jesse, Al, Charlie & the great Louis Farrakhan, make sure they have plenty of cash. They shake corporations down, they stir the racial pot until it is boiling and when it gets going really good, they retreat to their bank vaults to count their fortune. They lie big time, and just throw things out there and even when questioned, they are allowed to turn and walk away without any accountability for the untruths they have just tossed as reality. I don't think they would know reality if it bit them in the butt!

It makes me crazy.

So, no more long-term assistance programs! Any assistance programs must and will be monitored, why? Because, it is my money, that's why. I want a routine reconciliation. I have a right, I wrote the check.

CHAPTER 4
THE BIG WINDS CAME

Why did it seem that New Orleans was the only place that got smacked by the vicious storms this year. If I hear how bad New Orleans got hit one more time, I will throw up.

They were not the only ones who lost everything, I will say they were the only ones looting, crying poor me, pointing the finger at the President, as if he created the hurricane, and just flat out standing there waiting for you and me to come and get them and make it all better.

I know there are those of you who will say, "how can you say that, it was awful and people suffered? Yes, you are right; but, and this is critical, it did not have to end up like that. We have received an abundance of emails following the Katrina and Rita catastrophes. We all saw the pictures on TV, we heard and saw the looting, we saw those folks waving towels for us to come and get them. What part of Mayor Nagin's "Mandatory" evacuation and this storm is big and getting bigger" and we don't know if the levees will hold, did they not understand?

I don't know about you, but oh, I saw it coming. As the masses lined up, they began to grumble and complain as they stood in line for their turn into the Superdome. The rains came and it was now the 11th hour. Did no one think – hey, if "the big one" hits, we are going to be sitting in a very large stadium, with 10s of thousands of people who we don't know, in a structure unknown of its ability to withstand a potential Cat 5 storm.

Oh yes, I guess they did not think, humm, the power will most assuredly go out because of the storm, there will, in all probability, be no running water, so therefore sanitation systems within the dome will not work, and what if New Orleans' levees don't hold, what will happen outside, what will we eat and drink and for how long will we be stuck here.

The illustrious Mayor "Sugar" Ray Nagin did not bother to do anything proactive such as the humanitarian or thinking thing of having food, drinking water, a few necessities, medical people, the National Guard or Red Cross in there too!

Why should he, was he going to be there? I don't think so!!

Oh yes, and how about a caring Governor in Blanco, who stood stoically beside Nagin as he utters the word "Mandatory", shaking her head yes. Of course this would be the Governor who just recently spent millions of dollars to refurbish her offices for her and her staff, including flat screen TVs. Are they not supposed to be working at work, the people's business, making things better for all of her constituents she is now stealing from to make her surroundings posh? If I were her constituent, I would oust her in a heart beat for misappropriation of funds, when so many are still living in hotel rooms after the storm (of course this is because Ms. Blanco did not put together a plan to get them local FEMA trailers set up so they could return to their home base). By the way, we hear the trailers are just sitting there waiting meanwhile, you and I are writing big and bigger checks for folks to be hanging out in hotel rooms, with someone cleaning up after them, and I am sure we are feeding them too. What a life, where do I sign up Gov. Blanco. You most assuredly will be re-elected you have gone above and beyond job negligence!

Well, I take my hat off to our President, who in an unprecedented, proactive measure, called for States of Emergency for the several states in the storm's path in advance of landfall.

Now I know these poor folks had TVs, (some of them now have 4 or 5 extra big screens they acquired for free, AFTER the storm). (I know, I know, they were taking them to use to barter for food later,), anyway, they had to hear the warnings coming over the last 5 days prior to the storm's arrival.

They beat feet to the Superdome and partied on the booze and anything else they could put their hands on. Keep in mind - Most of them **CHOSE to stay!** Remember the word — Accountability, folks. They chose! So why did we have to pick up their panicked rear ends, and now all of the pieces because of their choices?

This is from General Chris Adams.

Compiled from various confidential sources.

On Friday night before Katrina hit the gulf coast, Max Mayfield of the National Hurricane Center took the unprecedented action of calling Mayor Nagin of New Orleans and Louisiana Gov. Blanco personally to plead with them to begin Mandatory evacuation of New Orleans, and they said they take it under consideration.

This after the NOAA buoy 240 miles south had recorded 68 foot waves before it was destroyed. Pres. Bush spent Fri. afternoon and evening in meetings with his advisors and administrators drafting the paperwork required for a state to request federal assistance — This for all of you who said he was enjoying his vacation and did not do anything.

Just before midnight Fri. evening the President called Gov. Blanco and asked her to sign the request papers so the federal government and the military could legally begin mobilization and call up. She told him that they didn't deem it necessary for the federal government to be involved yet.

After the President's final call to the governor, she held meetings with her staff to discuss the political ramifications of bringing federal forces. It was decided that if they allowed federal assistance it would make it look as if they had failed, so it was agreed upon that the feds would not be invited in.

Saturday, before the storm hit the President again called Blanco and Nagin requesting they please sign the papers requesting federal assistance that they declare the state an emergency area and begin mandatory evacuation. After a personal call from the President, Nagin agreed to order an evacuation, but it would not be a full mandatory evacuation and the governor still refused to sign the papers requesting and authorizing federal action. In frustration, the President declared the area a national disaster area before the state of Louisiana did, so he could legally begin some advance preparations. It is also reported that the President's legal advisers were looking in to the ramification of using the Insurgence Act to bypass the Constitutional requirement that a state request federal aid before the federal government can move into the state with troops, but that had not been done since 1906 and the Constitutionality of using it before the actual disaster was called into question.

The investigation also will have to look into why the emergency preparedness plan submitted to the federal government for funding and published on the city's website was never implemented and, in fact, may have been bogus and displayed only for the purpose of gaining additional federal funding.

We have just now learned that the organizations identified in the plan were never contacted or brought into any of the planning, though the document implies that they were.

The people of New Orleans should ask some hard questions (as, should we all) and they should start with why Blanco refused to even sign the multi-state mutual aid pact activation documents until Wednesday, which further delayed the legal deployment of National Guard troops from adjoining states. They should also ask why Mayor Nagin keeps saying that the President should have commandeered 500 Greyhound buses to help him when, according to his own emergency plan and documents he claimed, between the local school buses and the city transportation buses, he had at his disposal over 500 buses, but never raised a finger to prepare them or activate them.

As I watched the rains and wind hit New Orleans and the other abounding cities, the newscasters reported the best they could.

The next morning revealed that New Orleans seemed to make it through much better than the many cities of Mississippi and Alabama, although it was short lived, for soon the water seemed to start gushing in.

It seems to me the Mayor and Gov. said the levees were only meant to withstand a Cat 3, so this should not have been any big revelation that there were breaches and there certainly was a lot of water on the other side – no where to go, but into the city below sea level.

The stories began to filter out that the Dome did not fair too well, it had tremendous exterior damage which led to water coming in, but that exterior damage was nothing to compare to the now trashed interior of the once "super" Super Dome. It seems that during the storm, many of the New Orleans residents could not handle the stress. They were "driven" to tear up anything that was between them and the "free" liquor once locked inside. It drove them to party wildly, while some others who had no place to go and were now locked in the depths of the Super Dome, were forced to witness their antics in horror. Nothing would keep these folks, now in their deep distressed, alcohol driven state, from anything else they could put their hands on. I guess they forgot, they were guests and had been invited to stay at this facility since they did not leave town in the week preceding the landfall.

I don't know about you, but during a hurricane, **sex** would be the last thing on my mind. I don't know how many rapes actually occurred during this rampage, because the illustrious Mayor, told the world that there were tens of thousands of deaths, and the Superdome was filled with murdered victims and he did not even know how many rapes had occurred. IT seems the Mayor has a problem telling the truth.

People were outraged to hear this, and the federal government started getting as many people in as possible to help.

People demanded that the President order troops home to go in and restore order. I guess Mayor Nagin did not know his facts. I think the story goes that he was reliant on his sources for this information. Blame someone else! I guess he did not know that gangs from outside New Orleans were planning on everyone being out of town, because they had boats and came in and started breaking in and taking anything they could get their hands on, others planned with them and joined in the fun! From Nikes, to guns, jewelry, money, big screens, they had a holiday of taking. They then shot at those trying to get in to help, they looted anything and everything they could get to, and it is even said that policemen dropped their shields and had at it too.

Do you think that any of these caring individuals will be brought to justice? I want to know if Nagin has what it takes to seek all of these people out and put them behind bars forever. How despicable is this?

There were instances where some who had no ability to make a choice, were left at the mercy of caretakers, and were then abandoned. The sick and the elderly were left to drown where they were. For each one of those poor folks, I cry and I know Judgment Day will be interesting for those who left them there.

Some viable social commentary I think.

There was an email circulating of George Carlin's comments on Hurricane Katrina in New Orleans and he offered a set of rules on dealing with hurricanes:

First of all it was a hurricane, NOT an earthquake. WE KNEW IT WAS COMING.

Rule #1. A mandatory evacuation means just that… Don't blame the Government after they tell you to go. If they hadn't said anything, I can see the argument. They said get out… if you didn't, it's your fault, not theirs.

Rule #2. If there is an emergency and you plan not to evacuate, stock up on water and non-perishables (and rubber rafts). If you didn't do this, it's not the Government's fault you're starving and wet.

Rule #2a. If you run out of food and water, find a store that has some. He reminded everyone that shoes, TVs, DVDs and CDs were not edible and to leave them alone!

Rule #2b. If the local store has been looted of food or water, leave your neighbor's TV and stereo alone. (See #2a)

Rule #2c. If you're one who subjected your children to this disaster by staying in New Orleans, putting what you wanted to do before their safety, then you need to be prosecuted for endangering their lives.

If you are a person who stole non-edible items in front of your children then you should be prosecuted for contributing to the delinquency of minors. And if your child was hurt, became ill due to the conditions or died during this disaster, then you should be executed.

Rule #3. If someone comes in to help you don't shoot at them and then complain no one is trying to help you!!!

Rule #4. If you are in your house that is completely under water odds are your belongings are too far gone for anyone to want them so saying that is the reason for staying put is ridiculous.

Rule #5. My tax money should not pay to rebuild a 2 million dollar house, a sports stadium or a floating casino. Also, my tax money shouldn't go to rebuild a city that is under sea level. You wouldn't build your house on quicksand would you?

Rule #6. Regardless of what the Jessie Jackson and Al Sharpton want you to believe, the US Government didn't create the hurricane as a way to eradicate the black people of New Orleans and the Russians didn't do it as a way to destroy America. The US Government didn't cause global warming that caused the hurricane. For crying out loud, we've been coming out of an ice age for over a million years!!!

Rule #7. The government isn't responsible for giving you anything. This is the land of the free and the home of the brave, but you gotta work for what you want. McDonalds and Wal-Mart are always hiring, get a job and stop spooning off the people who are actually working for a living.

Rule #8. This situation was the fault of your state's power-hungry Governor (remember she didn't want to admit she wasn't in control and hand things over to FEMA and the National Guard) and your proud Mayor. The year after he was elected your Mayor took ALL the $4.5 million in emergency funds allocated to assist New Orleans' residents in just this type disaster and used them to teach minority kids to play sports. So if you're up to your waist in muck and starving, ask a kid with a basketball for some assistance because he is the one that got all the money for just such an emergency.

So there you have what has been sent around the world, blunt, yes, true, well you make the call!

To the lady who arrived in Houston after our rescuers got her out, who actually ripped off her sunglasses, and shrieked that Mr. Bush should remember her and all that "he" put her through, I say, Hummmmm and what did you do for yourself????

President Bush, there are those of us who know you did what you could by putting people in jobs who were to be responsible for doing their jobs, but unfortunately, they either did not do their job or were kept from doing their jobs by the choices and down right poor decisions of the like in Mayor Nagin & Gov. Blanco.

Remember folks, these two were voted into office, they, get and got big bucks to do a job that they ultimately failed at miserably when it counted most.

I will say one thing, I have never seen two people point fingers so quickly and neither one would ever step to the plate and say they made a mistake. Gov. Blanco did get to work on one thing. It took her staff 6 months to get the emails all together so we would all know what REALLY happened per her office. Where were the emails? The staff must have called Al Gore to help them on the Internet. It took 6 months to make them tidy enough for us to read? We were not born yesterday folks. It wasn't that it took them 6 months to glean out the truth so they would not be seen for what they were and are – inept!

I don't know about you, but if I ever messed up like that on a job, I would not have that job for long… Hint; don't allow these two back into those offices you voted them into. They do not deserve another chance.

Well their poor job costs plenty and for the money that was spent to go in after them and clean up their mess, we could have used those billions to actually start rebuilding the city already, but no we will and are, writing a bigger check for both.

Why? Because people don't listen, and people make stupid decisions, and people are just LAZY!

We heard that one excuse for the folks not leaving New Orleans was no transportation! This makes me ponder, because it is said that there are over 200,000 vehicles having been turned in for insurance claims?? I just don't think the numbers mesh folks.

Of course Mayor Nagin would have gotten the remaining thousands out of town, but he could not get the air conditioned buses he felt were required, and he did not want to put these poor people through riding on rinky-dink school buses. So now we have hundreds of school buses lost to the floodwaters, buses that could have been saved, if he would have used his head and not been so arrogant!

Get out another check friend; we have to replace those buses now too. This did not have to be!

My heart aches for the children. They did not ask to be born, and they certainly did not choose parents who did not put their safety first. They did not have control over where they were taken. Their parents, obviously cannot do what is needed to assure their safety, because if they did, these poor kids would not have had to go through this. Some parents were even so kind as to hop a bus and leave without the kids. This was the reported case of 6 children found wandering in the disgusting water filled streets of New Orleans, (the oldest was reported to be six and was carrying his infant sibling), but it was ok, Mom was safe and had found her way to San Antonio. I don't know about you, but it would be a very icy cold day in Hell before I would leave my children or grandchildren. I guess she would have realized they were missing when she had to produce a head count to get her full share of the money being handed out!

We keep hearing the poor were abandoned, well it was done by their elected officials in Gov. Blanco and Mayor "Sugar" Ray Nagin, who were busy playing - Tug of war, with power. These two would not even allow the Feds to come in, but boy oh boy, when the writing was on the wall, they were the first to step up and start blaming whom???? The President, the Federal government, you and me, everyone but the right ones – where is their accountability? I guess it blew away with the storm.

Just like Mighty Mouse, the Federal government finally did arrive and save the day! Now of course, it was too little, too late, per Nagin, Blanco, Kennedy, Rangel, Farrakhan, and any other liberal who had nothing to do but to rant and rave and wanted FEMA's Brownie out! Ya need a scapegoat when you failed at your own responsibility, it is the American Way, I guess. Brownie may not have been perfect, but in my humble estimation, he was no worse than anyone else those following days.

A job that should have never cost what it did, entailed what it did, and became what it did, all started with 2 people not doing what was right, and what they were paid to do. I am not kidding, if they were waiting for my next vote, they would be waiting until you know where freezes over!

Two other states were hit and hit hard, but did you see them pointing at the President, blaming the President, blaming the Federal government or having to rely on other people to risk their lives to save them, one by one, hundred upon hundred? The answer is no!

In fact, these people in some cases lost entire cities, and it was days before you even heard or saw their devastation. Why? I think it had to do with the fact that if you are not poor, black and or stupid, you are not newsworthy!

Mississippi and Alabama lost whole cities, whole revenue producers, some people died there too, but most of them were not poor or black and it would not make us feel as guilty if we were shown too much of them.

CHAPTER 5
I ALWAYS WANTED TO VISIT HOUSTON, TX!

I have said it before and I will say it again, I think Mayor Nagin has a problem telling the truth. He had to make it sound bad, really bad, so Mighty Mouse would come in and save the day.

We saw the rescuers - people from all over the US dangling from helicopters. These people were hovering amongst many perils, slipping and sliding on roofs trying to cut through roofing to save people trapped inside. Hundreds of people owe their lives to these unselfish people.

Ok, we have saved their lives, now they want a ride out of the town they did not see the need to leave earlier. Many demand to be taken out, they don't ask and they want out NOW!

Houston, and many other cities opened their doors, hearts and wallets. The state of Texas should get a big round of applause. Those people really have big hearts and started the ball rolling. I take my hat off to your willingness to offer your hospitality.

I am not sure they knew what they were going to get for all of their hospitality though.

The following story was witnessed by a friend of ours.

At the state line between Texas and Louisiana, there is (was) a huge, new rest area. It is or should I say was, nice.

When the first batch of evacuees were loaded up and on their way to Houston, a gentleman, who works for the Texas DOT, answered a call for Texas DOT employees to go help with the evacuees who were coming to the rest stop. After working <u>All Day</u>, this gentleman and three other associates from his office, left for the state line at I-20 and Waskom, TX. Working that evening was a State Trooper, several Sheriff's office deputies, Red Cross workers, Texas DOT employees and other local volunteers. The buses from New Orleans start pulling in. They let the people off to use the facilities. As they get off the bus, they are greeted and shown to the various areas of the rest stop. These poor, poor evacuees (cannot use the word Refugees, per the Rev. Jesse Jackson) were certainly appreciative! They proceeded to show their appreciation by urinating all over the walls, floors, mirrors, etc. No need to flush the toilets, that would necessitate exerting themselves or showing some civility! It did not stop there. They visited the local Burger King and were given (free) hamburgers and hotdogs and again many volunteers were so very willing to serve those who had been through so much. It will make you so proud to know that two dudes – I know you will be surprised - African Americans, were so humbled by this, their grateful response was," Man, I don't want none of that shit." Other volunteers were handing out bottles of water; the people would take them, drink two or three swallows and throw them on the ground. Volunteers spent hours and their own money, making up snack bags for the less fortunate, only to watch as these so "grateful" folks would dig out what they wanted and throw the remainder on the ground. These fresh BRAND NEW FOOD ITEMS were donated and packaged as an act of kindness and brotherly love. Anyway, these volunteers, who on their own time, after long days of work, had to now pick up the garbage that these ingrates left behind. They ended up hauling off two very large truckloads of trash from poor, poor distraught folks.

I am sure there will be some of you saying, this cannot be true, but the acquaintance of ours lives in Shreveport, LA, just 20 miles from this rest stop. She was by there a few weeks later, and the rest stop was still closed, the truckers can only park and rest there, the bathrooms and other portions of the rest stop were still under "renovation"!

In Houston there were nice clean beds, hot food, showers, tons of clothes and what is this???? Free money! Riots broke out at the Astrodome when the word got out that someone was giving away $2000 FEMA debit cards. The Red Cross was giving some too, but they were not the "big ones", no they were willing to fight with their fellow evacuees, as they tried to get the "Free money", free money that we owed them for all they had been through.

It's ok, they are so distressed that they need the thousands of volunteers to cook for them, clean up after them, get their kids in school or better yet, take them off their hands and watch them so Mom can get a reprieve from all of this free stuff!

I don't know about you, but the only free meals we have ever gotten were the MREs we stood in line to get after Hurricane Ivan. This went with the water and ice that we also stood in line for, but truly, truly appreciated. We actually opened and fixed these meals according to the directions and they tasted so good, especially since it was all we had, and we appreciate it.

These folks waited for the next meal to be cooked, they took their free bus rides to places like designer hand bag stores to drop $800 of their $2000 debit cards, WE gave them, on a designer handbag. I don't know about you, I probably will go to my grave without ever having a designer handbag. Ya just have to know how to do it, I guess!

I watched Fox News and there was one guy who was complaining about the debit cards. He said that the card cut him off at $700 and that it was not activated for the rest. I suspect he did not know that maybe he did not have the $2000 card, since there were debit cards given out by other organizations for lesser amounts to be used to buy essentials.

Anyway, the newscaster asked him what did he want or need? He demanded that each of them should be given at least ——- hang on to your seat now – at least $20,000 for now. He then began to use very profane language and they cut away.

He will get it and more if Gov. Blanco and her cronies like Landreau, who has written a Bill outlining $251 Billion to rebuild and bring people back to New Orleans. That equates to $55,000 to each man, woman and child that had lived there.

Excuse me, first of all, a great number won't come back, they have found an easier life in Houston or one of the other shelter states and it is just too much trouble to move back and we are still picking up the tab for a cushy hotel room and whatever else they are still demanding. So then you have those who should have had insurance. I know, I know, the poor did not, but the businesses had to have. So how much money do we have to give on top of the insurance claims being paid and what we have already given? This just does not make sense!

I have to tell you after Ivan, my husband and I had to write the big check ourselves, our insurance deductible was 5% of our home value, and our damage did not top it, so WE WROTE THE BIG CHECK FROM OUR BANK ACCOUNT!

We also had to drive 50 miles one way, to sit in line for gas, only to have it run out before we got ours, so on to the next station to start all over again. There were no stores with electricity or goods for weeks, so we ate MREs or drove the round trip of 100 miles for food, which you did not do, because you had to save the gas and make each trip count.

After a year, there is still a sea of blue roofs (Corp. of Engineers gave you the plastic until you get your roof fixed) in the Pensacola area. You don't hear much about that do you?

Our Governor told us to leave, told us what to expect when we returned and had the water and food as close as possible, but it took weeks to get back up and to begin to assume a new normal, because nothing was ever the same normal again.

You have to be patient, you have to do what you are told, and you have to help each other. You stand or sit in long lines, you make countless phone calls to insurance companies, and calls to repairmen, and then you have to wait for them to appear.

You won't believe this, but I was shocked, I could not see anyone in Alabama or Mississippi on TV in fistfights over "free" money or looting their neighbor. No they patiently stood in line, made their own phone calls to insurance companies, or went to where the insurance companies had set up shop to begin their process. Oh gosh, did I say insurance again? That's right, normal people try to do the right thing and protect themselves by having insurance. Silly people, we could have just let everything be blown or washed away and let someone else pay for it – Isn't that the way it is done???

My heart goes out to those who did the right thing, and came back to nothing, may they be blessed with a better home, and better jobs and better LIFE! They have earned and deserve it. The story has been reported to be the same from everyplace the majority of these poor evacuees have gone. They got off the buses and were greeted with food, water, clothes, etc. and, the thanks, in many cases, was to abuse the help and destroy the surroundings.

Comments to volunteers, "Is this all you got to give me"?, and the proper use of a trashcan has not been learned, even by the eldest of them. Oh yes, now do we see why the majority of places these poor, distraught folks seemed to congregate, looked like a PIG STY when they departed. A thought comes to me – they know you and I will clean it up! You know -the new slaves, us!

We, with the help of our elected officials created this monster!

It is said that the media did not report the whole story. Probably true, especially the liberal side, what they cannot find bad, they make up.

The following story was circulated in emails about a girl who lives in Louisiana and amid all the turmoil there reported. "We have had a battery operated TV so we've been getting local channels focusing on the situation there and here. I am just getting the national perspective and it's ticking me off. First, this is not a racial thing. I am sorry if all the reporters are seeing are black faces but if they would take their cameras to places like Slidell, Mandeville, Metairie and Chalmette, they would see several thousand white faces being affected by this. Most of the tip of the boot that is Louisiana south and east of Baton Rouge is under water. Those people are stuck too waiting for help, dying, but all the news people can focus on is the Superdome.

She further went on to say that the violence going on there is not the reaction to desperate people, it's typical New Orleans on any given Tuesday.

It's a dangerous, dirty, drug infested place where the city police and city government is corrupt and useless. Volunteers are getting shot at and their cars vandalized. Helicopters are being shot at, she said, just another day in the city of New Orleans.

Another misconception. These poor people couldn't get out because they don't have cars. If the cameras show the city once the waters recede you will notice all the flooded out cars littering the streets. They couldn't all have been broken down before the storm hit. Yes there are always people who do not have transportation. Part of making the call for a "Mandatory" evacuation is that the city has to provide for transportation and/or shelter in the city. People stay for the same reasons they always stay. They think the storm will turn and go in another direction. The think they can "ride it out". Or they just are to *&^% lazy to pack up and leave.

Another misconception. The federal government was slow to respond. The President issued a state of emergence BEFORE the storm ever hit, unprecedented. This means that the full access of the federal government, be it military or civil, were at our governor's disposal.

The levee broke early Monday afternoon. Gov. Blanco did not call evacuation until Tuesday morning. You cannot call up National Guard units in 20 minutes. It takes time. The governor and mayor are in high CYA mode at the moment.

The situation is bad here. Crime is becoming a problem in Gonzales and Baton Rouge where the evacuees are being housed. We live between the two cities and there is a pistol now on my desk shelf as I type, and yes I know how to use it.

Helicopters are flying overhead all day, gas is running out, stores shelves becoming empty. It is like a war zone. Pray for us."

The emails we alone have received following this disaster are disturbing. Some were funny, some were not, but they all served as a wake up call to me. Like this one.

What I learned about the Hurricane:

Things I have learned from watching the news on TV during the last 8 days —

The hurricane only hit black families' property.

New Orleans was devastated and no other city was affected by the hurricane.

Mississippi reported to have a tree blown down.

New Orleans has no white people.

The hurricane blew a limb off a tree in the yard of an Alabama resident.

When you are hungry after a hurricane steal a big screen TV.

The hurricane did 23 billion dollars in improvements to New Orleans. Now the city is welfare, looters and gang free and they are in your city.

White folks don't make good news stories.

Don't give thanks to the thousands that came to help rescue you, instead bitch because the government hasn't given you a debit card yet.

Only black family members got separated in the hurricane rescue efforts.

Ignore warnings to evacuate and the white folks will come get you and give you money for being stupid.

I know there are going to be outraged screams over printing this, but do normal, hardworking people see truth here. You cannot argue, no matter how hard you cry foul, to dispute these findings — white, black, Mexican, or Asian — whomever the shoe fits!

CHAPTER 6
HEEEERE'S JESSE AND HIS GANG OF RENOWN

The Rev. Jesse Jackson said evacuees from the Gulf Coast are not refugees; a word he believes suggests sub humans or criminals. "It is racist to call American citizens refugees, he said".

From "The Houston Chronicle"

"Many black leaders have said that this (the response to Hurricane Katrina) is an example of black genocide."

A reporter at a Hurricane Katrina press conference held by the Congressional Black Caucus wrote this quote.

"There's going to be plenty of time to make (hurricane recovery) a racist issue, and I'm going to do it." Congresswoman Diane Watson responding to the question.

Ok, Jesse Jackson, and all of the rest of you who are stirring madly the pot of racism, you win. You figured it out. There's no keeping a secret from you and your fellow black leaders. So on behalf of the Vast, Right-Wing conspiracy, I will now confess all":

Hurricane Katrina was a racist.

"Katy" As we called her in the labs of Halliburton, Inc., was unleashed by the Bush Administration and its evil minions in the oil industry using a super-secret, high tech weather machine originally developed in the labs of Nazi Germany and passed down through the Skull and Bones Society at Yale. Just ask John Kerry, he knows all about it.

Of course Katrina, hit New Orleans and its predominately black population, and largely avoided the mostly white residents of the "Redneck Riviera of the Florida panhandle. Don't you remember how Katrina started out hitting Florida, then swung around the entire state in order to get a clean shot at the Big Easy? All part of the plan.

The folks in the congressional Black Caucus know. They know that Katrina (why not "Catherine?" No "K" of course) was created by the Bushies to accomplish two key goals, disrupt oil supplies so when the US finishes stealing all the black gold from Iraq, the prices will remain high, and kill lots of black people, who historically tend to vote Democrat, so the GOP can dominate the South.

Those blacks who didn't die were to be disenfranchised by being labeled "refugees: one of the most insulting and racist terms in the English language, so demeaning it has often been used in the past to describe Jews.

See how the conspiracy all fits together?

But the plan almost failed despite the best efforts of the weather masters at NASA, Katrina hit to the east of New Orleans, allowing the levees to hold. Then, suddenly, the levees failed nearly a day later. What really happened?

To find out, consider this questions from a sharp-eyed reporter at the Bush/Clinton hurricane aid press conference: "How do you respond to rumors that the levees were intentionally opened?"

Aha! Caught again! The levee system, which withstood the hurricane itself, had to be blown the next day, using a secret, silent explosive developed by the Pentagon for the Contras in Nicaragua back in the 80s, all funded by the CIA, thanks to profits from selling crack to inner-city blacks.

The levees were breached, and the city was flooded.

Next came step three: forcing all the rescue boats, trucks and buses to sit idle on the outskirts of New Orleans for a week, waiting for more black people to die.

Why, of course that's what happened. Oh, sure, you could blame FEMA's horrifically incompetent performance on the fact that the head of FEMA is a nitwit named Michael Brown, whose previous emergency management experience was running horse shows for the international Arabian Horse Association, a job he was forced out due to incompetence. But that the easy obvious answer the conspirators want you to buy.

Congressman Elijah Cummings of the Black Caucus saw right through that. The people in New Orleans could have been rescued, as he put it, in a snap, but they weren't because they were black. Instead, poverty, age or skin color, determined who lived and died in this storm. Cummings told reporters.

Hilary Shelton, head of the DC NAACP, was even more specific, "Boatloads of white Americans (were) taken away from New Orleans, while thousands of African-Americans were left behind".

In other words, Louisiana National Guardsmen, New Orleans cops (those who actually showed up for work or (weren't too busy looting local Wal-Marts) and Red Cross workers all were sitting in their trucks ready to go into the city, but waited patiently while FEMA managers told them, "Can't go in yet too many black people still alive! Let's wait until we get a few more floaters.

Some dismiss this theory as paranoid nonsense, pointing out that many of those Guardsmen, cops and volunteers were black, too, and would likely object to being part of such a murderous racist plot.

Ah, but I haven't told you about the Karl Rove Mind-Control Ray, now have I?

There's no reason to hide it anymore. Even rap stars like Kanya West have figured it out. George Bush doesn't like black people! Just ask Condi Rice, Rod Paige, or Colin Power. Air America's Randi Rhodes knows it. She said that Bush is happy when black people are dying. That why, Pres. Bush signed a bill, sending $10.5 billion hurricane relief, much of it going to black communities in Louisiana and Mississippi.

When members of the Congressional Black Caucus compare conditions at the Houston Astrodome to slavery; when Jesse Jackson, Jr. defends the right of looters to steal plasma TVs in order to eat (there's a recipe I'd like to have), when Randall Robinson reports that black hurricane victims in New Orleans have begun eating corpses to survive, (a recipe I'd rather skip), when these unfounded charges are repeated again and again, inflaming racial tension at a time of great national tragedy what these courageous leaders of America's black community are really saying is, "It doesn't matter how many million of white Americans send how many billions in aid and charity to those suffering along the Gulf, America is still racist and we know it! "You can't fool us!"

And I ask you in all honesty, who can argue with logic like that?

We can expect them to get started on the right track because the work ethic is still missing. There was a job fair in Shreveport a couple of weeks after the evacuees were taken out, only 20% of ALL the able bodied, old enough evacuees located in that area, turned up to apply for jobs. This is just one area and one example.

In Houston, as of the 12th of September 2005, the ones who are willing to work, get on and try to do the right thing have left the Astrodome, the rest; well you can figure it out. They were just laying on a nice comfy bed, with lots of blankets waiting for the next hot meal to be cooked, and served to them, then they would catch a free bus ride to anywhere in the city, and then there have been a few who just walk into convenience stores and take what they want – not to bother to pay for it because they are from New Orleans, and they don't have to pay for anything. This is a true account!

Jesse, Al, Charlie, where are you????

CHAPTER 7
GOD HELPS THOSE WHO HELP THEMSELVES!

How often have you heard that phrase?

I heard it a lot growing up. I don't think that it is repeated in certain realms though. If so you would not see the welfare or "entitlements" programs growing on a daily basis. I know I got into this before, but I love that term entitlements. Who put that label on these handouts or "free money" programs? Our hard earned dollars are taken away and just like Robin Hood, they take it and give to the poor. Of course, you have to remember who is choosing to enhance these so called entitlement programs, these are the people who will do anything for a vote, and who you won't find writing their big check, they write yours and mine!

I have watched the likes of Jesse Jackson, Al Sharpton, Louis Farrakhan, Harry Reid, Nancy Pelosi, Barbara Boxer say the most unimaginable things I have ever heard, and I guess the only thing that tops it is the fact that there are some idiots out there that actually believe them.

What they have managed to do in 3 weeks is to set human rights back 100 years. If the black community think these representatives are working in their interest, they had better think again. These 3 men alone amass millions of dollars in their personal bank accounts, not in their brethren's accounts. It would be a sad day to see white people doing this to each other.

Yes, Mr. Farrakhan, we white folk blew a hole in the levees in New Orleans, and then we wrote check after check, we sent our sons, daughters, spouses in the form of relief workers to feed them, bring them to safety, work tirelessly without thought to themselves to save lives. Really, I think you went completely over the top on that one. If we wanted to do anything like that, we would have done the job right the first time, and we would have taken the whole thing out. The other one that was really a hoot is that the Red Cross is too white – well, I guess if you really cared about your brethren of color, you would be there working with or for the Red Cross to help all of those less fortunate – black and white! You know they are always looking for volunteers, I would be blown away to see his illustrious self serving it up and helping instead of stirring up nothing but trouble.

But, who are the poor? Those who don't have, ok next question, why don't they have? The number one reason is because people like Al Sharpton, Jesse Jackson and Louis Farrakhan tell the blacks – hey, you don't have to be like the white folks, you are owed because way back when, your people were slaves, and so now you can make the white people take care of you. Sorry, this is garbage and does not compute! If you want to be taken care of, then get out there and do the right thing, and that does not mean taking what is not yours. Work for it the "old fashioned way", and if one job is not enough, get a second one, oh yes, and don't bother having more children than you can support yourself, because, no one else is going to do it for you. This was posted as a comment on a photo page...

It is insightful and very brave.

Welcome to the land of the free. Free to come and go as you please. Free to board up windows, free to ignore weather warnings, free to stand on the side of the road out of town with your thumb out begging for a ride, free to take your gas-less car to a gas station and beg for gas, free to wait for someone else to come save your ass, free to sit on that ass and pray to God for help. What ever happened to "God helps those who help themselves.??

Here again, in times of strife, the question on everyone's mind becomes: "Who is to blame?" Well I know the answer... I blame President for not calling you personally to tell you a HUGE hurricane is coming to your house and to leave the area.

I blame the Red Cross for not setting up a five star resort outside the predicted hurricane path 3 days before it hit and for not shuttling you there on a charter bus.

I blame the Mayor for not sending a limo to pick up your poor ass to get you out of town. I blame your mother for not smacking you upside the head more often as a child to knock more sense into you, and you for not smacking your stubborn mother when she said she wanted to stay.

I believe it's every President from Washington to Bush 43's fault for making you live below sea level in a geographic region prone to hurricanes. It's also his fault you are poor, have 4+ kids and no spouse, no car, gas, food water or scuba gear, but you do have gold chains around your neck.

It's his fault your welfare check can't afford you an Escalade or in this case a Zodiac with a 15 HP Johnson outboard to get your soaking wet ass off your tin roof.

(At least the folks in the tornado belt have the common sense to build tornado proof basements to hide in, well most of them, there are those mobile homes, that become flying projectiles when picked up by a 150 mile per hour wind.)

There are some people of this nation becoming weaker and weaker – always looking for someone else to blame for their own predicament. It is always someone else's fault. I am tired of people using socio-economic or "poor' as an excuse. "I can't feed my family 'cause I'm poor. I can't get a job, 'cause I am poor, I can't get an education, 'cause I'm poor. I can't (whatever), 'cause I'm poor". I grew up poor and busted my ass not to be poor.

This country gave me the freedom to do just that. I know that 99% of poor people are poor because they are just plain lazy or doped up on drugs or drunk "Poor" is a choice not an excuse!

What has happened to this area and the people in it is a tragedy. WE as a country should do what is reasonable to help them. But, before you go placing blame and pointing fingers at anyone else, point the finger at yourself (especially those of you waist deep in water) and ask yourself if you personally did everything you could to prevent that.......

Neal Boortz, replying to a Black writer (race baiter) who complained about injustice in New Orleans.

"You say that you're angry at your country for doing nothing when it mattered. Nothing???? Just, what country, Mr. Robinson, were those helicopters and rescue swimmers from, you know the ones I saw on Tuesday morning plucking victims, "black victims from rooftops". Did those helicopters make a supersonic flight across the Atlantic from the African continent to assist in the rescue effort?"

For the past three nights Mr. Boortz told of his family, his wife and daughter, working Red Cross and Salvation Army telephone banks. They were taking donations from Americans to help the victims of Katrina. They had to beg volunteers to go home because there were only so many telephones and more volunteers lined up to help.

He guesses that this Black writer did not see any of this because he was too busy seething with hatred for America to see all of those lining up across American looking for a way to help. The majority of those volunteers were white and the phone bank was deep in the heart of a majority black city. He said these were the Americans who Mr. Robinson said were "doing nothing when it mattered."

Millions of dollars were collected in this phone room in Atlanta in 60 hours! Nothing????

He pointed out that the helicopters show up at New Orleans hospitals to evacuate patients, and black predators in the street fire on the helicopters and the brave ones aboard. People showed up to help and blacks tried to murder them!

Friday afternoon they heard that blacks showed up outside the BellSouth building in St. Bernard's Parish. Inside that building were BellSouth employees who had been trapped there by the water. The black and white employees just wanted nothing more than to get out. Mr. Boortz asked Mr. Robinson, "Did the blacks you're so concerned about show up to help rescue the BellSouth Workers"? No they showed up to loot. They showed up to kill. They started firing on the BellSouth building and on the law enforcement personnel who showed up to help. He said there was word that one police officer was killed. I guess he was doing nothing to help!

The Super Dome and the New Orleans convention center had black predators roaming looking for rape victims, and petrified tourists were beaten.

Mr. Boortz asked Randall Robinson, that when helicopters, on rescue missions, were fired on by blacks, doctors and nurses in stranded hospitals, moved patients to higher and higher floors, as black looters invaded the floors below. Cries for help came from a children's hospital as black looters tried to break in from the streets. Police officers, attempting to make rooftop rescues, were fired on, by roving gangs of armed blacks.

Then there is Mr. Randall Robinson telling the world that blacks are having to eat corpses in New Orleans, because no one has come to help them.

Ok, I add Mr. Randall Robinson to the list of Jesse, Al, Charlie and Louis! He definitely threw it out there and just walked away. Thanks to Mr. Boortz, he was challenged.

My blood boils every time I read or see these things. Does the word LAZY and ungrateful come to mind?

So many volunteers were so dismayed by the wastefulness, what they got for so much of their hospitality and giving is, nasty, filthy mouthed, ungrateful and uncaring evacuees from New Orleans, who are now laying on cots in Houston, or one of many other unsuspecting shelters who opened their hearts, purses and lives to people who are laying on cots waiting for the next meal to be cooked for them, or the next announcement of when the next debit card will be issued. I personally think, and I am hearing I am not alone, that giving, giving, giving is the worse thing we should be doing.

Let's show them the way to the employment office, to the schools, to the technical training centers, teach them to volunteer of the time and energy.

Here are some interesting facts coming out after the Hurricane blew through. 75% of the residents of New Orleans evacuated before the hurricane and that left about 300,000 most were from the city's public housing projects, home of uncontrollable crime and irremediable squalor, allowed to be that way. We fix it up; they tear it up, time after time, after time. Get the picture!

Sorry Mayor Nagin, I think this falls in your job description, no plan for evacuating all of the prisoners in the city's jails, we hear that they were let out, of course many of these free folks came from the "projects".

There were many decent innocent people, some who were tourists; some who had no other way out were trapped in New Orleans when the storm passed through. They were now at the mercy of the pack of animals unleashed by the incompetent administration of New Orleans. This incompetent administration was working overtime. On what? you may ask.

Well, they were not going to Disneyland, but close. Mr. Nagin was planning a trip to Las Vegas for these overworked, unappreciated public servants and their families, while the rest of their fellow brethren were left knee deep in trash and water to be saved by the rest of us.

These public servants and their families had to be revived from all the tumult of this nasty hurricane.

Mayor Nagin in sending his first responders and their families to Las Vegas to party. Let's see, what did the Mayor say when questioned about his allowing this? I believe his own documented words were "That's what the people of New Orleans do, get over it"!

I don't know about you, but I have not gone to Las Vegas on your dime, and I doubt that you have gone on mine, but these strangers did. But now they have no money, the city is broke; we need $251 billion of your and my money. I don't think so!

Mayor Nagin ran on a platform of getting rid of corruption, corruption by the welfare state that has been allowed to thrive. I personally think he has done a tremendous disservice to his constituents.

The following is taken from the ITA Daily on September 2, 2005.

"What Hurricane Katrina exposed was the psychological consequences of the welfare state. What we consider "normal' behavior in an emergency is behavior that is normal for people who have values and that the responsibility to pursue and protect them. People with values respond to a disaster by fighting against it and doing whatever it takes to overcome the difficulties they face. They don't sit around and complain that the government hasn't taken care of them. They don't use this chaos of a disaster as an opportunity to prey on their fellow men.

What about criminals and welfare parasites? Do they worry about saving their houses and property? They don't, because they don't own anything.

Do they worry about what is going to happen to their businesses or how they are going to make a living? Why should they now, they never worried about those things before. Do they worry about crime and looting? No, they concentrate on living off of stolen wealth and this is a way of life for them.

The welfare state – and the uncivilized mentality it sustains and encourages — is the man- made disaster that explains the ugliness that has swamped not only New Orleans, but also the whole United States. We allowed it to come to be, and only we can make it go away."

I pray that the actions of Mayor Nagin, and many others in power like him, are remembered.

They are NOT to allow the murder, rape and looting that happened after this storm, to happen. You, Mr. Mayor and Ms. Governor, did not take good care of the people who put you in office or came to visit the city you were supposed to rule, to protect and lead them in time of peril.

We, the people, will and must stand up and let these "public servants" know that they rule at our discretion, and no more. We put them there and we can send them home.

I have been urging my friends and family members to write their members of Congress to tell them not to back the $251 billion Bill that the Louisiana leaders think we have to give them. This Bill is so full of stupid things they should be ashamed for even trying to push it through. I guess they thought, it always worked before, let's try it again. Well I am not going to list all of the crazy things contained in this Bill, but you can get a copy of it from Sen. Mary Landrieu's office, I am sure. It will blow your mind when you see what they want to use our tax dollars for in Louisiana in the name of rebuilding after Katrina. You should become fighting mad and write your Congressmen and tell them – No Way had they better push it through.

I did what I had urged my family & friends to do. I wrote and this is what I got back from Georgia Sen. Saxby Chambliss.

He thanked me for writing, and told of how this was the worst natural disaster in U. S. history and this thoughts and prayers went out to everyone.

He also informed me what our nation was doing. That we were working around the clock. There were more than 15,000 National

Guardsmen, 7800 U. S. Military personnel, 4000 U. S. Coast Guard personnel, more than 400 federal law enforcement officer and 61 FEMA response teams. Over 49,800 lives saved, 22.5 million meals and 53.3 million liters of water have been provided more than 500,000 evacuee families have gotten emergency help to pay for food, clothing and other essentials.

He went on to say that the long-term recovery efforts are being put in place to help families rebuild their lives. Congress approved $10.5 billion and aid package for the victims of Katrina, and a second aid package of $52 billion was passed on 9/8/05.

He further said that Matthew Jadacki, was going to be in charge of preventing potential problems of abuse and assure that disaster assistance funds are used judiciously.

Mr. Chambliss stated the over view of President Bush's address to the nation on 09/14/05 outlining the federal government commitments, which included 3 new commitments to meet the immediate needs of the evacuees.

One of them is $5000 to which each evacuees can draw upon for job training, education and child care during their search, I think this is a good one, as long as they can not have it unless they provide support documentation to back their draws on the $5000. Now this 3rd one is for Congress to pass the Urban Homestead Act., which says that property owned by the Federal Government will be provided to low income citizens free of charge while they in return and pledge to build on the lot. Now my quandary is how are they going to build, when they claim they have no money, they have no equity in what they left behind, where is that money going to come from to build? It was left unanswered.

Thank you sir for not telling me how you were going to vote on the $251 Billion dollar bill. I let him know I will be watching to see how he votes, but I have an idea, I am not going to be happy with the outcome.

CHAPTER 8
OKAY, WHY?

We must identify from this disaster, why so much of what has happened did occur. It did not have too, and my Conservative Right gut feeling says it was because the Democrats leading, supposedly, the program in New Orleans, could not do the job. The Liberals stirred the pot until it boiled, and once again told those who decided to take the easy way out, it was everyone else's fault but theirs.

Here is another one of the emails we received, I am sorry, but Bob Beckel and Alan Colmes, you won't like this, but...

Texas: Productive industrious state, run by Republicans.

Louisiana: Government dependent welfare state run by Democrats.

Texas: Residents take responsibility to protect and evacuate themselves.

Louisiana: Residents wait for government to protect and evacuate them.

Texas: Local and state officials take responsibility for protecting their citizens and property.

Louisiana: Local and state officials blame federal government for not protecting their citizens and property.

Texas: Command and control remains in place to preserve order.

Louisiana: Command and control collapses allowing lawlessness.

Texas: Law enforcement officers remain on duty to protect city.

Louisiana: Law enforcement officers desert their posts to protect themselves.

Texas: Local police watch for looting.

Louisiana: Local police participate in looting.

Texas: Law and order remains in control, 8 looters tried it, 8 looters arrested.

Louisiana: Anarchy and lawlessness breaks out, looters take over city, no arrests, criminals with guns have to be shot by federal troops.

Texas: Considerable damage caused by hurricane.

Louisiana: Considerable damage caused by looters.

Texas: Flood barriers hold preventing cities from flooding.

Louisiana: Flood barriers fail due to lack of maintenance allowing city to flood.

Texas: Orderly evacuation away from threatened areas, few remain.

Louisiana: 25,000 fail to evacuate, are relocated to another flooded area.

Texas: Citizens evacuate with personal 3-day supply of food and water,

Louisiana: Citizens fail to evacuate with 3-day supply of food and water, do without it for the next 4 days.

Texas: FEMA brings in tons of food and water for evacuees. State officials provide accessible distribution points.

Louisiana: FEMA brings in tons of food and water for evacuees. State officials prevent citizens from reaching distribution points and vice versa.

Louisiana: Media focuses on poor blacks in need of assistance, blames Bush.

Texas: Media can't find poor blacks in need of assistance, looking for something else to blame on Bush.

Texas: Coastal cities suffer some infrastructure damage, Mayors tell residents to stay away until ready for repopulation, no interference from federal officials.

Louisiana: New Orleans is destroyed, Mayor asks residents to return home as another hurricane approaches, has to be overruled by federal officials.

Louisiana: Over 400 killed by storm, flooding and crime.

Texas: 24 killed in bus accident on highway during evacuation, no storm related deaths.

Texas: Jailed prisoners are relocated to other detention facilities outside the storm area.

Louisiana: Jailed prisoners are set free to prey on city shops, residents, and homes.

Texas: Local and state officials work with FEMA and Red Cross in recovery operations.

Louisiana: Local and state officials obstruct FEMA and Red Cross from aiding in recovery operations.

Texas: Local and state officials demonstrate leadership in managing disaster areas.

Louisiana: Local and state officials fail to demonstrate leadership, require federal government to manage disaster areas.

Texas: Fuel deliveries can't keep up with demand, some run out of gas on highway, and need help from fuel tankers before storm arrives.

Louisiana: Motorists wait till storm hits and electrical power fails. Cars run out of gas at gas stations that can't pump gas. Gas in underground tanks mixes with floodwaters.

Texas: Mayors move citizens out of danger.

Louisiana: Mayor moves himself and family to Dallas.

Texas: Mayors continue public service announcements and updates on television with Governor's backing and support.

Louisiana: Mayor cusses, Governor cries, Senator threatens President with violence on television, none of them have a clue what went wrong or who's responsible.

Louisiana: Democratic Senator says FEMA was slow in responding to 911 calls from Louisiana citizens.

Texas: Republican Senator says, "when you call 911, the phone doesn't ring in Washington, it rings here at the local responders".

What if state and local elected officials were forced to depend on themselves and their own resources instead of calling for help from the federal government? Texas cities would be back up, and running in a few days.

Louisiana cities would still be under water next month.

Speaking of water – there was this one. Sen. Kennedy, in my personal opinion, the constituents of Massachusetts must only have one choice on the ballot, if not, they should be terribly embarrassed to offer this guy up again and again – is he the best they can come up with? He waddles up to the microphone, makes ridiculous statements, without any supporting basis, 99.5% of the time and walks away. This from the man who keeps most of his money, not where it can benefit the US and be taxed like the rest of us, but in various foreign accounts A man that can make the wife of a learned judiciary person named Samuel Alito weep, because of his ignorance and lack of purpose.

Sen. Kennedy was reported to have said the following: "What the American people have seen is this incredible disparity in which those people who had cars and money got out . . . and those people who were impoverished died." - Ted Kennedy on Hurricane Katrina

The response is... "Ditto" Remember Mary Jo Kopechne?

We have allowed people, with few if any, morals to take control. No more.

Robert Tracinski said, "It took four long days for state and federal officials to figure out how to deal with the disaster in New Orleans. The reason is that the events there make no sense if you think that we are confronting a natural disaster – not Bush made! If this is just a natural disaster, the response for public officials is obvious, you bring in food, water and doctors, you send transportation evacuate the people to a temporary shelter, you send engineers to stop the flooding and rebuild the city's infrastructure. For journalists, natural disasters also have a familiar pattern, the heroism of ordinary people pulling together to survive, the hard work and dedication of doctors, nurses and rescue workers, the steps being taken to clean up and rebuild. Public officials did not expect that the first thing they would have to do is to send thousands of armed troops in armored vehicles as if they are suppressing an enemy insurgency. The journalist, myself included – did not expect that the story would not be about rain, wind, and flooding but about rape murder and looting.

But this is not a natural disaster. It is a man made disaster.

The man-made disaster is not an inadequate or incompetent response by federal relief agencies and, this was not, directly caused by Hurricane Katrina. This is where just about every newspaper and television channel has gotten the story wrong.

The man-made disaster we are now witnessing in New Orleans did not happen over the days following the storm. It happened over the past four decades. Hurricane Katrina merely exposed it to public view. The man-made disaster is the welfare state.

For the past few days, I have found the news from New Orleans to be confusing. People were not behaving, as you would expect them to behave in an emergency – indeed, they were not behaving as they have behaved in other emergencies. That is what has shocked so many people; they have been saying that this is not what we expect from America. In fact, it is not even what we expect from a Third World country.

When confronted with a disaster, people usually rise to the occasion. They work together to rescue people in danger, and they spontaneously organize to keep order and solve problems. This is especially true in America.

We are an enterprising people, used to relying on our own initiatives, rather than waiting around for the government to take care of us. I have seen this a hundred times, in small examples (a small town whose main traffic light had gone out, causing ordinary citizens to get out of their cars and serve as impromptu traffic cops, directing cars through the intersection) and large ones the (spontaneous response of New Yorkers to September 11).

So what explains the chaos in New Orleans?

To give you an idea of the magnitude of what is going on here is a description from a Washington Times story:

"Storm victims are raped and beaten, fights erupt with flying fists, knives and guns, fires are breaking out, corpses litter the streets, and police rescue helicopters are repeatedly fired on."

The plea from Major C. Ray Nagin came even as National Guardsmen poured in to restore order and stop the looting, carjackings and gunfire.....

"Last night, Gov. Kathleen Babineaux Blanco said 300 Iraq-hardened Arkansas National Guard members were inside New Orleans with shoot–to–kill orders."

"These troops are under my orders to restore order in the streets, she said. They have M-16s, and they are locked and loaded. These troops know how to shoot and kill and they are more than willing to do so, if necessary and I expect they will."

The reference to Iraq is eerie. The photo that accompanies this article shows National Guard troops, with rifles and armored vest, riding on an armored vehicle. Through trash-strewn streets lined by a rabble of squalid listless people, one of who appears to be yelling at them. It looks exactly like a scene from Sadr City in Baghdad.

What explains bands of thugs using a natural disaster as an excuse for an orgy of looting, armed robbery, and rape what causes unruly mobs to storm the very buses that have arrived to evacuate them, causing the drivers to drive away, frightened for their lives? What causes people to attack the doctors trying to treat patients at the Superdome?

Why are people responding to natural destruction by causing further destruction? Why are they attacking the people who are trying to help them?

When the first pictures came in, New Orleans seemed to have escaped, and the parties began in the French Quarter, even without electric and water. They dodged the bullet!

The people wanted out, the people wanted food and water and to go to their homes.

Oops, but wait a minute, those pesky levees seemed to have sprung a leak and water was now pouring in and that bullet was not dodged.

Ok, down the road, we have Mississippi and Alabama, where the majority folks got out of Dodge", when they were warned to, even though they did not appear to be in the bull's-eye. Many miles were completely wiped out, nothing left, big and beautiful homes, long standing businesses – gone! They needed help too!

Do you know what I saw? I saw those outside of New Orleans beginning to come back to what had been home and work. They were dazed and in shock, there were tears, there was clinging to each other, but the big difference from New Orleans, you did not hear that anyone was partying on other peoples' liquor, you did not hear of rapes and murders, you did not see hundreds, if not thousands, breaking into other peoples' business grabbing jewelry, TVs, sneakers, and name brand clothing, and don't forget guns, bullets and booze and running full tilt from the same! No these people found strength to search for anyone that may have not made it out, they found shovels, wheelbarrows, started finding heavy equipment and ways to get "cleaning up".

Why so different? After last year's Hurricane Ivan, we in the Florida Panhandle area, and parts of Alabama, were also devastated, we lost a section of I-10, (which by the way after 16 months later, is still not repaired, but we noticed the other day that less than 6 months later the I-10 section was open in New Orleans, interesting) none of the bridges were deemed safe for several weeks. People living out on Santa Rosa Island in the Pensacola area could not get to their homes for weeks, both bridges had missing sections or cracks, and when they could go out, they had to walk, some as far as 20 miles, NO VEHICLE TRAFFIC WAS ALLOWED. We had to deal with it and we waited patiently.

Guess what! There were no rapes, no looters, no partying, there were tears by us all as we had to drive 50 or more miles to sit in hour long lines for gas, only to watch them sell the last drop and frantically drive to another station and begin all over again. Then sit in lines for water, ice and MREs, when we could finally get through on cell phones to our insurance companies, we had a lengthy process to go through, then you had to wait for the adjusters to arrive for their assessment.

You sat for several days waiting for running water, which you were told to boil, but oh by the way, there is no electric yet, you finally get electric and land line phone service, but there is no cable TV for weeks.

You were thrilled if you were alive, and had most of your home in tact, and you saw and heard the long lines of out of state help arriving. You still could not get local gas, the gas stations were either very much destroyed, or they had gas and could not pump it because there was no electric. There were no grocery stores, they were either badly damaged, but most of all, they like you, lost all of the perishable foods, and had to wait for trucks to make it in. It took weeks before we could even find milk, and still had to drive 50+ miles.

Remember I spoke about writing the big check out of our account because we had large deductibles – a percentage of our homes value, so now you find out that the deductible, ours was around $14,000 is a little higher than your damage, so even though you consider yourself very lucky to have your home, you have to write the big check out of your bank account to pay for the repairs. You write the big check and no FEMA, no Red Cross checks, no $2,000 debit cards.

We knew that those folks were helping those who had lost everything or nearly all.

There are some folks in Pensacola, whose land was worth the money, but their home was gone and they still had $400,000 or more in mortgage notes and no the insurance check would not even begin to cover rebuilding their home. The cost to rebuild doubled it seemed. The building Codes changed again, there was and still is a shortage of building supplies, and there was a shortage of people to do the work, which further pushed up the costs.

The strange thing in today's world is that the storms help the economy. You now have all of this need for building and furnishing homes, hundreds of thousands of them. You have a big demand in carpentry workers, a shortage of places to live, and the pricing for all of these things soared and continues to soar. The strangest of all outcomes was, that for us our property value rose over night. Even in a hurricane area, but houses were going within hours of being listed and you named your price, especially if it was undamaged. There were 4-5 offers at one time. It was crazy. It will be interesting to see what happens in New Orleans, but I imagine the same thing will happen in Mississippi, Alabama, Texas and the rest of Louisiana. As for us, the house went on the market when it was repaired and we got the heck out of Dodge!

The stories we heard in our area were heartbreaking, and you know what? No one had to bring in the National Guard, or helicopters to save thousands of people and waste all of that time, money and resources, so those funds were used to start rebuilding. Sounds like a big difference from New Orleans doesn't it?

Even 16 months later, take a ride through Pensacola and Santa Rosa Island, they are coming back, but there is still a great amount of devastation remaining and you have not heard or seen that on TV lately. No one getting killed, no one of color being neglected I guess. They are coming back, slowly but surely, and not begging for help. They sure don't get a pat on the back for being patient and self-reliant. No news worthiness there, I guess.

Sent: Wednesday, November 30, 2005 7:02 AM **Subject:** Dakota/ Montana Weather Bulletin …

For those of you who are not aware, North Dakota and southwestern Montana got hit with their first blizzard of the season a couple of weeks ago). This text is from the county emergency manager out in the western part of North Dakota after the storm.

Amusing… **WEATHER BULLETIN**

Up here in the Northern Plains we just recovered from a Historic event —- may I even say a "Weather Event" of "Biblical Proportions"

—- with a historic blizzard of up to 24" inches of snow and winds to 50 MPH that broke trees in half, stranded hundreds of motorists in lethal snow banks, closed all roads, isolated scores of communities and cut power to 10's of thousands.

George Bush did not come.... FEMA staged nothing.... No one howled for the government... No one even uttered an expletive on TV... Nobody demanded $2,000 debit cards.....

No one got re-located. No one asked for a FEMA Trailer House.... No Red Cross Assistance

No news anchors moved in.

We just melted snow for water, sent out caravans to pluck people out of snow engulfed cars, fired up wood stoves, broke out coal oil lanterns or Aladdin lamps and put on an extra layer of clothes.

Even though a Category "5" blizzard of this scale has never fallen this early...we know it can happen and how to deal with it ourselves. Everybody is fine.

THAT'S BECAUSE NO ONE CALLED JESSE JACKSON AND LOUIE FARRAKHAN!

CHAPTER 9
GOVERNMENT OFFICIALS AND HOW THEY GET INTO THOSE NICE POSTIONS

We elect people into jobs to represent us. They staff up on people they like, they owe, or they trust to cover their behinds, and so on.

My husband and I have seen people get high-level jobs who did not have a clue about what to do or how to do it. Sometimes they are lucky enough to find people who will do their bidding and make them look good, so they get to stay there and even move higher.

I have witnessed GS14 or GS15 persons, come to GS6 level employees to seek their help in completing a task given to the higher grade. The employee would attempt to show them, only to get the "never mind, you will just do it for me, right?" You are my can do person! The higher-level person did not have a clue! Should they not have the knowledge on how to do those things they are responsible for overseeing? Not in the government? Later I found, not necessarily in the private work arena either.

I sometimes got a little tired of making other people look good when I was sitting there after 5 p.m. doing their work, or doing a job that a minority could not or would not do, but I was expected to do because!

Was I going to say no? My mama did not raise a fool, and I wanted to eat, so I did the job, gave it to them, they took it and presented it as their own and got a nice bonus or a promotion. WHAT DID I GET? I GOT HOME LATE!

The same goes for all of the other can do people out there.

These elected people are supposed to work for us and they have passed laws mandating that we MUST have a certain number of certain colors, genders and ages. If we don't we can get in real big trouble. Well, there are jobs that people are not qualified for. What a disservice you are doing to those by putting them in these jobs? Everyone loses, but most of all, the individual in the job. Maybe they will be lucky enough to find someone to always make them look good, but eventually, you and I pay a horrible price for that.

We have seen corporations and the government buckle to the shakedowns by people like Jesse Jackson.

What happened to a person having a job because they were actually qualified, not for what someone could scare you into thinking had to occur?

What happened to the fact that if you did a poor job, you were given a chance to clean up your act and if you did not, you were out looking for another job?

Why do you have to tolerate and spend your stockholders' or your fellow taxpayers' money to keep an unskilled, inept person in a job they could not, would not or cared to do?

Why is it that if your boss felt you did not perform according to the outlined job description, he can not put it in writing to, hopefully, help you get back on track or to at least keep you from being pushed upward into something you would be even more poorly qualified for? The boss cannot do this without fear of some kind of stupid legal suit, or worse yet, the boss is reprimanded because he may cause his employer to be sued.

What has happened? I don't know about you but I am tired of living in fear, or handing over my hard earned dollars to someone who is not willing to work and do what is right, or who thinks we owe them. I am tired of listening to self appointed "leaders" of the black community spin life to make it sound like every black person is owed by everybody for what nobody did to them.

There are people within the government who were administrative assistants. i. e. secretaries or receptionists, who all of a sudden had a new job title of "analysts". Only the Good Lord knows why, but I am sure the reason would make me angry, but worse yet, now they get paid more money for that new title and they take an attitude, because of what they now are.

Now nothing had changed in their actual job description, but these, and everyone I heard about were black, decided they no longer felt they should answer a phone, and no longer were going to type, so in essence changed their own job description because they did not feel like they had to, and you can not touch them. So now we pay more money for less, and an attitude. They were allowed to do this because we feared, or at least someone in a higher level did. We know of those who would come to work, when they felt like it, wearing house slippers and sit in their cubicle, with their TV on (can not miss that soap opera), and, hold on to your seat – healing people over the phone! That is right, healing – and they were not ordained by God, I don't think. You can not say anything, you just go to your office as a very high level GS grade to answer your own phone, type your own memo, and listen to this GS 7 – Analyst, heal unknowns on the other end of her phone on your dime! This is factual, and it is happening today.

Getting steamed yet? You should be. This is a terrible injustice to those who are placed in these positions, and it is unbelievable, that the ones who propose caring and equal rights, has served up a dish of setting people up to fail. Do you think these people should feel good about screwing us? No the ones being screwed are the ones in the jobs, because this is as good as it gets. Maybe, if someone who says they are helping them because they are owed, or don't have to work like everyone else, had helped them get more education, had taught them that by dressing right, abiding by the rules and actually working while at work, would help them become more upwardly mobile and more successful. They could feel good about themselves, they could be somebody, because they did it on their own and not because it was, mandated by law because of the color of their skin or that they were a woman, or that they were over 40, or whatever.

There are many stories, true ones, about high level government workers being drunk on the job by 11 a.m., using their power to give cash awards to people who had loaned them money, or done some other bail out for them. If you or I did that, we would be behind bars. There is no accountability and not enough checks and balances.

Now we hear that some law enforcement agencies will be allowed to hire folks even after known drug history. That scares me! I am not a prude, but the last I heard drug use is against the law, enforce the law, don't hire known lawbreakers. We cannot be that hard up in finding good dedicated people to fill these jobs.

People are sneaking across our borders because it is too much trouble to do it the right way. They use our medical facilities – they have no insurance, you and I pick up the tab, they bring diseases, they bring their drug habits, some steal, murder and rape, you see many have very lengthy rap sheets, and yet we are not enforcing the laws that are in place. We don't need to write more laws, just enforce the ones we have. I don't think we have to hire all Spanish individuals to use in some border areas, now don't get me wrong, I know they can speak the language, but don't you think they may be a little biased when trying to take them into custody? How many people are "allowed" to sneak over? We cannot afford any more of this nonsense. We can force our government officials to enforce the laws we have. Don't let them talk in circles and point fingers when all they have to do is allow the border patrol agencies, and re-enforce it if needed with Reserves or National Guard people. They are trained, they get paid anyway, let them earn it and the benefits we pay anyway.

There are government officials who have done things like write bad checks, use their job for their own personal gain, write off personal expenses on your dime, and they take great glee in exposing others among themselves, but I do believe, the majority of these officials, if put under a microscope, would not pass the "clean test".

We have to make it so they cannot abuse the office and their position. I would never abuse my expense vouchers, I would never disguise a trip for me and my family as "being on the job" as I skied down the slopes, or visited the Eiffel Tower, but this happens every day and has for decades. There is no accountability, no checks and balances in place. We need to demand it and if they won't allow it, or flags go up and no one does anything, - Bye, have a good life and good luck in your next job, are the words that should be echoing.

How about GS Grade 15, who lied about his education on his SF71, no one checked or verified. Just so you know, you actually have to sign indicating that the information contained is "factual & true", he did. He was allowed promotion after promotion, thanks to oh so many "can do people" along the way, and worst of all, he was an idiot. He skated through his good government job for his 20 years, arriving or getting drunk at his good government desk routinely, and never doing a lick of work, being caught using someone else's badge when his had been taken away, is still allowed to retire on the good government dime and live a pretty cushy life on us for however many years he has left. Sad isn't it!

More of our good hard earned money being spent so very wisely.

I love going into the post office. I get to stand in line, like a line of cattle waiting to be slaughtered, watch as the one of maybe 2 postal clerks manning the desks, slowwwllllllyyy does what he or she has to do, and you wait, and wait. Then when you get to them, they treat you like you are some kind of scum.

Hey, I write your check. I don't want an attitude, when you are supposed to be giving service for which I am paying way, way too much for and the cost is now going up 2 cents more a stamp. I don't think so.

You wonder how they ever passed the test! I guess like everything else now, we have numbers of who has to be hired, and if they don't qualify, we just lower the bar until they do.

The following was written by Lewis Napper, a self-described amateur philosopher and from Mississippi who ran for a U.S. Senate seat in 2000 as a Libertarian: "We the sensible people of the United States, in an attempt to help everyone get along, restore some semblance of justice, avoid more riots, keep our nation safe, promote positive behavior, and secure the blessings of debt free liberty to ourselves and our great-great-great-grandchildren, hereby try one more time to ordain and establish some common sense guidelines for the terminally whiny, guilt ridden, delusional, and other liberal bed-wetters. We hold these truths to be self evident: that a whole lot of people are confused by the Bill of Rights and are so dim they require a Bill of NON-Rights.

ARTICLE I: You do not have the right to a new car, big screen TV, or any other form of wealth. More power to you if you can legally acquire them, but no one is guaranteeing anything.

ARTICLE II: You do not have the right to never be offended. This country is based on freedom, and that means freedom for everyone not just you! You may leave the room, turn the channel, express a different opinion, etc.; but the world is full of idiots, and probably always will be.

ARTICLE III: You do not have the right to be free from harm. If you stick a screwdriver in your eye, learn to be more careful; do not expect the tool manufacturer to make you and all your relatives independently wealthy.

ARTICLE IV: You do not have the right to free food and housing. Americans are the most charitable people to be found and will gladly help anyone in need, but we are quickly growing weary of subsidizing generation after generation of professional couch potatoes who achieve nothing more than the creation of another generation of professional couch potatoes.

ARTICLE V: You do not have the right to free health care. That would be nice, but from the looks of public housing, we're just not interested in public health care.

ARTICLE VI: You do not have the right to physically harm other people. If you kidnap, rape, intentionally maim, or kill someone, don't be surprised if the rest of us want to see you fry in the electric chair.

ARTICLE VII: You do not have the right to the possessions of others. If you rob, cheat, or coerce away the goods or services of other citizens, don't be surprised if the rest of us get together and lock you away in a place where you still won't have the right to a big screen color TV or a life of leisure.

ARTICLE VIII: You do not have the right to a job. All of us sure want you to have a job, and will gladly help you along in hard times, but we expect you to take advantage of the opportunities of education and vocational training laid before you to make yourself useful.

ARTICLE IX: You do not have the right to happiness. Being an American means that you have the right to PURSUE happiness which, by the way, is a lot easier if you are unencumbered by an over abundance of idiotic laws created by those of you who were confused by the Bill of Rights.

ARTICLE X: This is an English speaking country. We don't care where you are from; English is our language. Learn it or go back to wherever you came from!

(Lastly...) ARTICLE XI: You do not have the right to change our country's history or heritage. This country was founded on the belief in one true God. And yet, you are given the freedom to believe in any religion, any faith, or no faith at all, with no fear of persecution. The phrase IN GOD WE TRUST is part of our heritage and history and if you are uncomfortable with it, TOUGH!!!!

If you agree, share this with a friend. No, you don't have to, and nothing tragic will befall you if you don't. It's just about time common sense is allowed to flourish. Sensible people of the United States speak out because if you don't, **insensible people will!**

CHAPTER 10
WAKE UP CALL

Wake up people who have been labeled as "the poor", you are being used by those who portray to want to help you.

They are only adding to the racist issue, they are only lining their own pockets.

I have a tremendous respect for Bill Cosby. He has gone out on a limb; he tells his people if you want to be respected, pull yourselves up. You have to do something to earn it. Thank you Bill!

Ya know though, Jesse, Al, Charlie and whoever else like them, hate Bill Cosby, why? Because he tells the truth, he was not given anything, he did not demand, he became educated, he worked hard, and maintained a sense of humor through it all.

This is my optic, but now when he tries to save his fellow brethren, the likes of those who like to make money off the man made plight, — their fellow brethren, lie about Bill, they try to trash him. Isn't this a sad state of affairs and I have to say it is - dirty pool, guys. How do you sleep at night?

I am not racist, I just feel the numbers speak for themselves, and when people like Bill Cosby tell the black population, you need to get educated, and you won't get respect or anything else by trying to stand out in stupid ways. A few examples are outlined in this email we received. Mr. Cosby, I think you are right on!

We Can't Blame White People — by BILL COSBY

They're standing on the corner and they can't speak English.

I can't even talk the way these people talk:

Why you ain't, Where you is, What he drive, Where he stay, Where he work, Who you be..

And I blamed the kid until I heard the mother talk. And then I heard the father talk. Everybody knows it's important to speak English except these knuckleheads.

You can't be a doctor with that kind of crap coming out of your mouth.

In fact you will never get any kind of job making a decent living.

People marched and were hit in the face with rocks to get an education, and now we've got these knuckleheads walking around.

The lower economic people are not holding up their end in this deal. These people are not parenting. They are buying things for kids. $500 sneakers for what? And they won't spend $200 for Hooked on Phonics.

I am talking about these people who cry when their son is standing there in an orange suit.

Where were you when he was 2? Where were you when he was 12? Where were you when he was 18 and how come you didn't know that he had a pistol?

And where is the father? Or who is his father?

People putting their clothes on backward: Isn't that a sign of something gone wrong? People with their hats on backward, pants down around the crack, isn't that a sign of something?

Or are you waiting for Jesus to pull his pants up?

Isn't it a sign of something when she has her dress all the way up and got all type of needles [piercing] going through her body?

What part of Africa did this come from? We are not Africans. Those people are not Africans; they don't know a thing about Africa.

With names like Shaniqua, Taliqua and Mohammed and all of that crap, and all of them are in jail.

Brown or black versus the Board of Education is no longer the white person's problem. We have got to take the neighborhood back.

People used to be ashamed.

Today a woman has eight children with eight different 'husbands' — or men or whatever you call them now.

We have millionaire football players who cannot read. We have million-dollar basketball players who can't write two paragraphs.

We as black folks have to do a better job.

Someone working at Wal-Mart with seven kids, you are hurting us.

We have to start holding each other to a higher standard. We cannot blame the white people any longer."

Thank you Mr. Cosby, and please keep it up!

CHAPTER 11
ATTORNEYS, LAWYERS, SHYSTERS, BARRISTERS OR LAW SCHOOL GRADUATES

The Trustees for the Colony of Georgia in 1735 declared the following:
Labor, Clear and Fence the Land,
Guard against the Enemy,
Set Self Up with Craft,
Plant Mulberry Trees Upon 50
Acres and Other Such Crops
Hard Liquor, Such as Rum,
Forbidden,
No Slavery,
No Unlicensed Trading with the
Indians,
No Lawyers in the Georgia Land.

King Henry VI, Part II
Charleston South Carolina

King Henry is quoted as saying: "The First Thing We Do, Let's Kill All The Lawyers".

The following information is the opinion of the writer and is based upon personal observations and experiences. It is intended for educational purposes and no negative information is intended.

These people must have had a good reason for the negative feelings and advice they passed on to us regarding Lawyers.

First lets examine what a Lawyer is and is not.

Lawyers go to school to become a "practicing" attorney. Some make it – some do not. Usually, when a person says he went to law school and is fixing cars or works at a dry-cleaners for a living, it means he did not pass a "test" (bar exam) to qualify to "practice law". Therefore, he is not a "practicing" attorney; he is a "Law School Graduate".

Law School – There is more that one type of Law School. One is a recognized as an ABA (American Bar Association) School, the other is not.

There is a pecking order associated with Law Schools. Some students go to school at night and some go to school in the daytime. Some go to law school three years and some go four years.

NORMALLY:

Three years in the daytime – ABA School.

Four Years at night – Not an ABA School.

The Bar Exam: It varies state-by-state regarding who takes the Bar exam: Each state has individual requirements: Example – California, New York, Florida or Illinois and some other states require a written test. Iowa requires that you lived in the state for two years.

I had a friend, who, as a minor child (3 to 7 years old) resided in Iowa with his parents. Based upon that residence he was permitted to practice law in the state of Iowa, as he had graduated from Law School. No written test was required. If you don't meet the requirements you don't practice law, ergo, we have what we call "Law School Graduates".

There is a myth floating around that Lawyers are brilliant – probably started and perpetuated by attorneys, but it is not necessarily true.

Lawyers conduct the "practice" of law in restricted areas or specialties – all lawyers are not a "jack of all trades". They usually practice law in specific areas such as Criminal Defense Law, (Criminal violations such as murder, assault with a deadly weapon, Grand Theft, (Forgery, Arson), Civil Law, (Divorce, Estate Planning, Wills), Real Estate Law, Banking Law, Administrative Law, Securities Law, Commodity Law, etc. These attorneys are called "private" attorneys as they function in a "Private Practice".

Then you have Government Attorneys. Some lawyers are not required to pass the bar upon employment and are usually given a "grace period" to pass a bar in the geographical jurisdiction where they are "practicing" law (usually two years).

They do not prosecute or defend but, "practice" or Pontificate law in areas of the government such as Agriculture, Commerce, Labor, Housing and Urban Development, the Environment, Education, or Veterans Affairs, some sort of Government cabinet organization, position or regulatory agency.

These folks (Government Attorneys) perpetuate themselves at your expense. Did you ever look at the Biographical data of a "head" of a Government Organization? If he/she is a Law School Graduate it seems that they hire (or surround themselves) with more attorneys. Why does an attorney need an attorney??? They say it is to give an objective view of different situations (AKA Spin). The truth of the matter, as I see it, is they hire attorneys to perpetuate the profession (again and again) at your expense.

Did you ever try to file a document in a court of law (a public forum)? You can't! They will tell you that you need an attorney.

The Government also hires prosecutors, public defenders, and other people to "run" the Justice System. They control it and they made it what it is.

Many media people have come to realize in recent years, after many public trials that "the system is broken". Examples of this broken system are the "O.J. Simpson Trial", and the "Michael Jackson Trial". Look at the analysis of these trials after the fact, they were run by attorneys. Did you know that Judges are attorneys also? Who are not necessarily bright people but were able to pass a written exam (bar exam or test) and get "an appointment to the Bench" through political connections.

One of the dumbest decisions I am reminded of continually when I drive by a US Government Facility is the waste of taxpayer dollars – caused by a judge. There was a trespassing trial where some individual entered a government facility by climbing over a fence. The judge ruled that the intruder was not guilty, as the government had not posted the facility with no trespassing signs, and ordered they be placed every 50 feet. NOW - you tell me how stupid you must be to enter a facility by climbing a fence. I suggest you must (in my opinion) be stupid to make such a ruling that costs the taxpayer exorbitant amounts of money because some dumb fool climbed a fence. Did the Judge or the violator think the fence was put there to be climbed or to keep people out? And the taxpayer keeps on paying.

Lets examine the truth. A government prosecutor and his supporting cast of Law Enforcement assistants is bound by the truth to prosecute a case – BUT a defense counsel can put any "spin" on a case and is allowed to present theory to win his/her case. This "practice" is placed under the guise of living up to the Code of Ethics to provide a good defense to/for your client. Today that equates to "I can lie in Court and if I win good for me and my client" – the defendant. OR - - you can witness "the race card being played".

People witnessed a very prominent black attorney play the race card continually and win his cases. Why – you ask – well racism is alive and well on both sides of the fence. Some minorities (both Judge and Jury) will not convict a person of the same color or race in a court of law based upon their false distrust of the court system. Prosecutors in the Nations Capitol will try to locate a friendly venue other than Washington, D.C. as a jury in Washington D.C. will not convict a defendant, as they do not trust a government case, despite the evidence.

Is this a message that the judicial system needs to be overhauled or what – BUT is anything happening to overhaul or fix the system – NO, and you and me – the taxpayers, keep paying the bill for these non-actions.

Why do individuals become attorneys? POWER?

They feel that knowledge of the law is power, control and knowledge over the "common man". You will note that attorneys love to argue just to prove or win a point. If you ask an attorney to answer a question you will usually get his/her opinion and not what the law says. We hire them, why, because we need them to tell us what the law says.

Judges rule based upon their opinion, not necessarily what the law says, that is why we have two types of law – Statutory law and Case law. Case Law is an offshoot of Statutory law and by judges making a decision based upon information they interpret from Statutory law. The Statutory law is known law, such as, you can not rob a bank, but Case law is made when a Judge would say that because an intruder was only half way into your house, he is only half guilty... Some of these judges get into criminal's intent – What?

If he was coming into my house, I think his intent was to break the law by breaking in, I don't care why and neither should the Judge. You would be surprised what some of these Judges have been delivering lately though. Definitely, their interpretations (Case Law), not as described by Statutory Law. When a child molester gets 60 days for a sentence after he had been molesting a child for over 3 years, some thing is wrong with the system. Yes, this was recently the sentence given by a Vermont Judge because he did not feel that the CRIMINAL would get help if he sent him away for a longer period of time, and besides, he no longer believed in punishment! This is a travesty, what about the little girl, whose life is now ruined, what is she – a nothing, no help can give her back what this monster robbed, and as far as I am concerned, there are two criminals here – the perpetrator of the crime, who confessed, and the remarkable Judge. This sentence did not fit the crime, which is what the LAW states it must do.

I have personal knowledge of two individuals who recently divorced in a state, which splits the property down the middle – yet the attorneys (both of them) kept telling their clients they were "entitled" to so much more and of course the bill is adding up. The law was clear, they were each entitled to half, no more and no less. These 2 lawyers stole, as far as I am concerned, large sums in fees, when the 2 people were going to only get what the state allowed, which is what happened. Lesson - If you live in a state where the property is split 50-50 in a divorce (known as community property) make sure you know it or the attorney can usually milk your wallet until it is dry.

When you are seeking to hire an attorney ask what the law is pertaining to the issue at hand– not what they think. When you want to get the facts about an issue pull the law up on the Internet – read it and compare what you are being told. The attorneys use West Law as their guide. You can go to the Library or use the web to research yourself.

Attorneys will tell you about the word "INTERPRETATION". Do you know what the word "is" is? Your former president, (AKA Slick Willie), an attorney, tried to beat an impeachment by putting a spin on the word "is". For the most part we know what something says. If a package says poison we understand that. If a law says a person is unable to care for himself or herself, we understand that. We understand "thou shall not kill". We don't need some attorney to "decipher" the word "kill" or "is" or whatever they want to fight over – at your expense. Also some attorneys will make up an answer to sway the deciding party to believe they know what they are talking about and what the law says. To avoid this from happening, ask the attorney what "section of the law" their theory or statement is connected to. Read the section yourself to insure that the statement or response is correct, and in compliance with the written statute or law.

Attorneys can lengthen cases/situations that in turn perpetuate the need for them and put money in their pockets.

Lets look at the Death Penalty in the State of California. The appeal process, designed by attorneys (and judges) can drag on for 25 to 30 years. The process involves frivolous appeals, motions and legal actions. After this is completed/exhausted the sentence is usually carried out.

These attorneys spend years having you pay for their activities and then just walk away from it all (after they have been paid from the tax coffer).

Recently a convicted killer appealed his case (thru an attorney) to the governor of the state. The governor took the matter under consideration, also his buddies in the movie industry got into the action. The movie folk, who obviously needed a cause for some camera time used the media to try and turn the tide against the execution. Now you tell me what a high school graduate who "played" a doctor on a TV series knows about the law – I think nothing. If this person is against the death penalty then use the influence he thinks he has to try to change the law via a legal process to stop the death penalty. Pay an attorney to go through the legal system and do something productive in the people's interest as he obviously sees it.

This "TV Doctor" said on an international TV show that the trial was flawed, the evidence was flawed and the convicted killer should not be killed based upon that. His suggestion was to let the convicted killer remain in jail for the remainder of his natural life. Not a very bright person, in my opinion. The trial was flawed, but keep him in jail anyways according to the "TV Doctor". Now I ask you, does that make sense???

How many of you know who the "Founding Fathers" are? How many of you know when the last Founding Father passed from this earth?

Well let me assure you that there is not an attorney alive today who knows or ever met any one of the Founding Fathers, yet time after time you will hear them say "the Founding Fathers intended". Do these luminaries have a telephone line hidden to wherever the Founding Fathers are located? The next time you hear an attorney (or Politician) say "what the Founding Fathers intended was", Folks bend over, Grab your socks, assume the position as the person who said that is going to stuff it to you again. Remember this – NO ONE KNOWS WHAT THE FOUNDING FATHERS INTENDED – EXCEPT – THE FOUNDING FATHERS and it was put in writing in our Constitution and Bill of Rights. What a concept, Huh?

Have you ever had someone say they are going to read your mind and be right?

If they do and are correct it's because they know you and yet these attorneys are reading minds of people they never knew or even met. What you also need to be careful of is when you hear an attorney (or politician) say, "I Opined" - That means you are getting a piece of these individuals' "Opinion". Opinions are like Onions – Most of them stink. (Opined = Grab your Socks – See above for further instructions.)

THE LAW IS THE LAW

So if the United States government determines that it is against the law for the words **"under God"** to be on our money, then, **so be it.**

And if that same government decides that the **"Ten Commandments"** are not to be used in or on a government installation, then, **so be it.**

I say, **"so be it,"** because I would like to be a law abiding US citizen.

I say, **"so be it,"** because I would like to think that smarter people than I are in positions to make good decisions.

I would like to think that those people have the American public's best interests at heart.

BUT, YOU KNOW WHAT ELSE I'D LIKE?

Since we can't pray to God, can't Trust in God and cannot post His Commandments in Government buildings, I don't believe the Government and its employees should participate in the Easter and Christmas celebrations which honor the God that our government is eliminating from many facets of American life.

I'd like my mail delivered on Christmas, Good Friday, Thanksgiving & Easter. After all, it's just another day.

I'd like the US Supreme Court to be in session on Christmas, Good Friday, Thanksgiving & Easter as well as Sundays. After all, it's just another day.

I'd like the Senate and the House of Representatives to not have to worry about getting home for the "Christmas Break." After all it's just another day.

I'm thinking that a lot of my taxpayer dollars could be saved, if all government offices & services would work on Christmas, Good Friday & Easter. It shouldn't cost any overtime since those would be jus! it like any other day of the week to a government that is trying to be "politically correct."

In fact.... I think that our government should work on Sundays (initially set aside for worshipping God...) because, after all, our government says that it should be just another day....

What do you all think????

If this idea gets to enough people, maybe our elected officials will stop giving in to the minority opinions and begin, once again, to represent the 'majority' of ALL of the American people.

SO BE IT...........

Please Dear Lord,

Give us the help needed to keep you in our country!

Amen and Amen

Touche!

These are definitely things I never thought about, but from now on, I will be sure to question those in government who support these changes.

This is not only about color, there are many people of all colors among us who find it easier to steal from their neighbors than to get off their lazy rear ends and get a job and earn it. Taking a life means nothing to many. Satisfying their sexual appetite at the expense of a small child, or any human being, as they could not help it, they had a poor childhood, they have a sickness or I love this one, a moment of insanity. Of course, what sane person would do such a thing, not once, but do it multiple times. The numbers would astound you.

The worst part is that we have people on the bench who could turn the tide, but don't. Many because they too are bullied by the fear of reprisal, fear of not being re-elected, so liberal they have lost sight of the victim's rights, who have now become over shadowed by criminal's rights. I guess it is a criminal justice system, because if you are the victim, you may be up a creek looking for justice. We need to get these robed liberals off their high seat and make them accountable for their decisions. If they allow sexual predators and murderers out of jail, they pay the price.

It makes me crazy, and it should make you crazy too.

Tuesday, October 04, 2005

The Color of Crime
By Nicholas Stix http://mensnewsdaily.com/blog/stix/2005/10/color-of-crime.html

Imagine if one demographic group in America were 33 times more prone to commit crimes than another group. How would you feel about the relatively crime-prone group? The relatively crime-free group? Wouldn't you want to know about such differences?

But we don't have to imagine anything. The above contrast was not a hypothetical case, but rather the statistical relationship of black to Asian crime in America, as detailed in the groundbreaking new report, The Color of Crime, released by the New Century Foundation, the organization that sponsors American Renaissance magazine.

"Between 2001 and 2003, blacks were 39 times more likely to commit violent crimes against whites than the reverse, and 136 times more likely to commit robbery."

Between 2001 and 2003, blacks committed, on average, 15,400 black-on-white rapes per year, while whites averaged only 900 white-on-black rapes per year.

"Of the nearly 770,000 violent interracial crimes committed every year involving blacks and whites, blacks commit 85 percent and whites commit 15 percent."

But there are five-and-one-half as many whites as blacks. If anything, the numbers should be reversed. After all, as leftists always tell us, all groups are supposed to be equally represented in all categories, for good or ill. (Well, not really. Leftists never call on the NBA and NFL to institute racial parity for white players.)

Nationally, youth gangs are 90 percent non-white. "Hispanics are 19 times more likely **than** whites to be members of youth gangs. Blacks are 15 times more likely, and Asians are nine times more likely."

The only crime category in which Asians are more heavily represented than whites is illegal gambling.

"Blacks commit more violent crime against whites than against blacks. Forty-five percent of their victims are white, 43 percent are black, and 10 percent are Hispanic. When whites commit violent crime, only three percent of their victims are black."

But how can that be, when for years commentators of all political persuasions have insisted that the majority of the victims of black crime were themselves black? But it has been true for some time, because blacks increasingly target whites based on the color of the latter's skin. The commentators have been guilty variously of lying and laziness.

Far from being guilty of "racially profiling" innocent blacks, police have been exercising racial bias on behalf of blacks, arresting fewer blacks than their proportion of criminals". Blacks who committed crimes that were reported to the police were 26 percent less likely to be arrested than people of other races who committed the same crimes."

"Police are determined to arrest non-black rather than black criminals." (I have seen **this** practice in operation on the streets and subways of New York.)

"[Blacks] are eight times more likely than people of other races to rob someone, for example, and 5.5 times more likely to steal a car."

Well, as everyone knows, innocent blacks get rounded up by the police, all the time, so we can safely ignore such statistics. After all, isn't that what the NAACP, Village Voice, New York Times, and countless black "activists" and prominent academics have been saying for years? After all, although the folks insisting on racial profiling have no facts to back up their claims, they enjoy political prestige and moral authority.

The Color of Crime, meanwhile, is based merely on lowly facts. As we shall see, prominent people are already saying that we should ignore

The Color of Crime, because it wasn't produced by the right sort of people. (And of course, "the right sort of people" doesn't tell the truth about race and crime.)

Charges of racial profiling, which maintain that police target innocent black motorists for traffic stops notwithstanding, a 2002 study by Maryland's Public Service Research Institute found that police were stopping too few black speeders (23%), compared to their proportion of actual speeders (25%). In fact, "blacks were twice as likely to speed as whites" in general, and there was an even higher frequency of black speeders in the 90-mph and higher range.

"The only evidence for police bias is disproportionate arrest rates for those groups police critics say are the targets of bias. High black arrest rates appear to reflect high crime rates, not police misconduct."

"Blacks not only commit violent crimes at far higher rates than non-blacks, but their crimes are more violent than those of whites. Blacks are three times as likely as non-blacks to commit assault with guns, and twice as likely as non-blacks to commit assault with knives."

"Blacks not only commit violent crimes at far higher rates than whites, but blacks commit "white collar" offenses — fraud, bribery, racketeering and embezzlement, respectively — at two to five times the white rate."

"The single greatest indicator of an area's crime rate is not poverty or education, but race and ethnicity. Even when one controls for income and education, the black crime rate is much higher than the white rate."

Things are actually much worse than the above notes suggest. As The Color of Crime notes, the feds inflate white crime statistics by counting Hispanic offenders as white; at the same time, "Hispanics are a [hate crime] victim category but not a perpetrator category. If someone attacks a Mexican for racial reasons, he becomes a Hispanic victim of a hate crime. However, if the same Mexican commits a hate crime against a black, he is classified as a 'white' perpetrator. Even more absurdly, if a Mexican commits a hate crime against a white, both victim and perpetrator are reported as white." Thus, the number of white perpetrators is bloated, while the number of white victims is constricted by the federal double standard.

But things are even worse than the study shows. It fails to note, with black-on-white male prison rape an institutionalized sport among black inmates, that hundreds of thousands of white men have thus been victimized but never counted by the government. Meanwhile, white-on-black male prison rape is virtually non-existent.

Some of the study's many sources were the FBI's uniform crime reports (UCRs); the feds' National Crime Victimization Study (NCVS), in which 149,000 people across the country, in statistical proportion to all demographic groups, were called; the National Incident-Based Reporting System (NIBRS); Supplemental Homicide Reports (SHRs); State Court Processing Statistics (SCPS); National Youth Gang Survey; Federal Justice Statistics Program (FJSP); and National Corrections Reporting Program (NCRP). The succinct report slays dragons in the course of mere footnotes, such as its nailing of tenured California State University criminology professor Phyllis B. Gerstenfeld, who in her book "Hate Crimes: Causes, Controls and Controversies", the reality of interracial violence be damned, depicted whites only as perpetrators, and not as the victims of hate crimes.

The Color of Crime - not to be confused with a 1998 piece of propaganda of the same name by tenured University of Maryland professor of criminology, Katheryn K. Russell — is the most scientifically, rigorous research on crime and race available. It's the state of the art.

The mainstream media will surely be anxious to publicize and discuss The Color of Crime. After all, hasn't the public been inundated since the late 1990s (and ultimately, since the 1960s) with dubious charges of racism ("racial profiling") against law enforcement and the justice system? And doesn't the MSM always tell us that they will report on anything newsworthy? After all, the New York Times claims to be "the newspaper of record."

In a future column, we shall see just how the MSM has responded to The Color of Crime.

In any event, the report gave in precise numbers what any sentient being over the age of twenty and living in the United States has long known. A 75-year-old Irish neighbor of mine is a retired nurse who was run out of a once-lovely Brooklyn neighborhood forty **years ago**

by "integration" (read: brazen black crime in broad daylight). During a friendly conversation during a quiet morning on our peaceful street last spring she said, "The problem is, you know what the problem is."

Just think if we did not have all of this crime, and the fear that goes with it, people could be educated to better their lives, have real family units, and be productive instead of wasting our money. Do you know what we spend catching, prosecuting, rehabilitating (which does not happen) and feeding, clothing and giving them a nice warm, clean cell with TV, computers, etc, and taking care of all of the kids and significant others they leave behind on the "outside". Enough, the stats speak for themselves.

Your honor, please make some examples of these people so more don't follow in their footsteps!

CHAPTER 12
THE MEDIA

It won't be easy for us to help our country to stand tall and proud again, but the Media could certainly help instead of hindering. The Fair & Balanced few cannot carry it all, but the Liberal Left can be brought back to center, IF we all make them. Stop buying those papers you cannot trust. Don't watch the news station that you have factual proof does not deliver the truth. If we cannot believe them, we don't need them and we can make them change their presentation away from their biased presentation to the true reporting of long ago. We can hurt them in the wallet. Trust me, they will change.

Following are things that make you think a little and I believe worth reading no matter what you think of our President!

There were 39 combat related killings in Iraq in January. In the fair city of Detroit there were 35 murders in the month of January. That's just one American city, about as deadly as the entire war-torn country of Iraq.

When some claim that President Bush shouldn't have started this war, state the following:

- a. FDR led us into World War II.
- b. Germany never attacked us; Japan did. From 1941-1945, 450,000 lives were lost ... an average of 112,500 per year.
- c. Truman finished that war and started one in Korea. North Korea never attacked us. From 1950-1953, 55,000 lives were lost ... an average of 18,334 per year.

d. John F. Kennedy started the Vietnam conflict in 1962. Vietnam never attacked us.

e. Johnson turned Vietnam into a quagmire. From 1965-1975, 58,000 lives were lost ... an average of 5,800 per year.

f. Clinton went to war in Bosnia without UN or French consent. Bosnia never attacked us. He was offered Osama bin Laden's head on a platter three times by Sudan and did nothing. Osama has attacked us on multiple occasions.

g. In the years since terrorists attacked us, President Bush has liberated two countries, crushed the Taliban, crippled al-Qaida, put nuclear inspectors in Libya, Iran, and North Korea without firing a shot, and captured a terrorist who slaughtered 300,000 of his own people.

The Democrats are complaining about how long the war is taking. But ..It took less time to take Iraq than it took Janet Reno to take the Branch Davidian compound. That was a 51-day operation.

We've been looking for evidence for chemical weapons in Iraq for less time than it took Hillary Clinton to find the Rose Law Firm billing records.

It took less time for the 3rd Infantry Division and the Marines to destroy the Medina Republican Guard than it took Ted Kennedy to call the police after his Oldsmobile sank at Chappaquiddick.

It took less time to take Iraq than it took to count the votes in Florida!!!!

Our Commander-In-Chief is doing a GREAT JOB!

The Military morale is high!

The biased media hopes we are too ignorant to realize the facts. But Wait. There's more!

JOHN GLENN (ON THE SENATE FLOOR) Mon, 26 Jan 2004 11:13

Some people still don't understand why military personnel do what they do for a living. This exchange between Senators John Glenn and Senator Howard Metzenbaum is worth reading. Not only is it a pretty impressive impromptu speech, but it's also a good example of one man's explanation of why men and women in the armed services do what they do for a living.

This IS a typical, though sad, example of what some who have never served think of the military.

Senator Metzenbaum (speaking to Senator Glenn): "How can you run for the Senate when you've never held a real job?"

Senator Glenn (D-Ohio):

"I served 23 years in the United States Marine Corps. I served through two wars. I flew 149 missions. My plane was hit by anti-aircraft fire on 12 different occasions. I was in the space program. It wasn't my checkbook, Howard; it was my life on the line. It was not a nine-to-five job, where I took time off to take the daily cash receipts to the bank."

"I ask you to go with me … as I went the other day… to a veteran's hospital and look those men …with their mangled bodies .. in the eye, and tell THEM they didn't hold a job!

You go with me to the Space Program at NASA and go, as I have gone, to the widows and Orphans of Ed White, Gus Grissom and Roger Chaffee… and you look those kids in the eye and tell them that their DADS didn't hold a job.

You go with me on Memorial Day and you stand in Arlington National Cemetery, where I have more friends buried than I'd like to remember, and you watch those waving flags.

You stand there, and you think about this nation, and you tell ME that those people didn't have a job? What about you?"

For those who don't remember .. During W.W.II, Howard Metzenbaum was an attorney representing the Communist Party in the USA. Now he's a Senator!

If you can read this, thank a teacher. If you are reading it in English thank a Veteran.

The more I have talked about writing this book, the more I am finding out I am not alone. There are many of us that feel that way, but feel helpless to do anything. I cannot and will not just sit and think out loud at home anymore. We have members of Congress standing before the media bad mouthing our Commander in Chief while we have troops in harms way, telling us we need to get out. Our President lied! (He did not and there is plenty of proof to back it up – to those mouthing horses, I say show me the "beef", I know you don't have it.

They say we have no plan for after the war. These people are fools in my estimation. The plan is keeping the terrorists from our shores, and helping Iraq to put together a Constitution, having elections, rebuilding schools, getting the economy back up and running, what is that chicken feed? What have you big mouths brought to the table? Nothing, nada, zilch!

Where is the respect they should be showing as a representative for us? I did not send them there to say these things on my behalf, on my dollar and to show disrespect to the office of President and our troops. How dare they! They are the biggest traitors I have ever seen and should be tried for treason. I know they have the right to say whatever they want, but not on the job that we are paying them to do. Go write a book, most of you have not had any problem doing that on my dime either, promoting it as well, on my dime.

Just remember, you will have to show proof in that book, unless you call it what you are living lately – Fiction!

IF it is not the war, it is Social Security, which supposedly per the liberal democrats, is not in trouble. We can recite many instances of where when it served their cause, was in fact in dire straits, but when our President and Republican party wants to try to fix it while they still can, are steam rolled. I can hardly wait for the next election. Every Democrat, and I am telling you now, will start claiming the past administration has done nothing to the now in shambles Social Security program. It will be mandatory that they get back in office to fix it. I ask you ahead of time, to make note, they have to have some sort of platform, none of the ones they have been throwing out lately are sticking, so all of a sudden – the Revelation – Social Security is fallen and it can't get up unless you let the Democrats/Liberals have a stab at it.

Just wait. We have been down this road before.

We thought we would share the following with you.

Dear Friends:

Many years ago in Seattle, two wonderful neighbors, Elliott and Patty Roosevelt came to my home to swim on a regular basis. They were a great couple full of laughter and stories that today I continue to marvel at.

Both are now deceased, but their stories remain. During the years of our friendship we had many, many discussions about his parents (President Franklin D. and Eleanor Roosevelt) and how his father and mother never intended for the Social Security and Welfare programs to turn out the way they are today.

Elliott used to say that if his mother returned to earth and saw what the politicians had done to their programs she would have burned all of them in hell.

Here is a story I received today regarding the Social Security Program and I immediately thought of Elliott's comments. Hope you will read this and think about it.

Margaret, Franklin Roosevelt, a Democrat, introduced the Social Security (FICA) Program.

He promised:

That participation in the Program would be completely voluntary,

That the participants would only have to pay 1% of the first $1,400 of their annual incomes into the Program,

That the money the participants elected to put into the Program would be deductible from their income for tax purposes each year,

That the money the participants put into the independent "Trust Fund" rather than into the General operating fund, and therefore, would only be used to fund the Social Security Retirement Program, and no other Government program, and,

That the annuity payments to the retirees would never be taxed as income.

Since many of us have paid into FICA for years and are now receiving a Social Security check every month — and then finding that we are getting taxed on 85% of the money we paid to the Federal government to "put away," you may be interested in the following:

Question: Which Political Party took Social Security from the independent "Trust" fund and put it into the General fund so that Congress could spend it?

Answer: It was Lyndon Johnson and the democratically- controlled House and Senate.

Question: Which Political Party eliminated the income tax deduction for Social Security (FICA) withholding?

Answer: The Democratic Party.

Question: Which Political Party started taxing Social Security annuities?

Answer: The Democratic Party, with Al Gore casting the "tie-breaking" deciding vote as President of the Senate, while he was Vice President of the U.S.

Question: Which Political Party decided to start giving annuity payments to immigrants? AND MY FAVORITE: Answer: That's right! Jimmy Carter and the Democratic Party.

Immigrants moved into this country, and at age 65, began to receive Social Security payments! The Democratic Party gave these payments to them, even though they never paid a dime into it!

Then, after doing all this lying and thieving and violation of the original contract (FICA), the Democrats turn around and tell you that the Republicans want to take your Social Security away! And the worst part about it is, uninformed citizens believe it!

If enough people read this, maybe a seed of awareness will be planted and maybe good changes will evolve. Maybe not, some Democrats are awfully sure of what isn't so.

CHAPTER 13
I AM NOT AFRAID ANYMORE

I champion those that work and try. We use to feel that we just had to take it – Guess what, I am no longer afraid!

Because, I am telling you now, I am not afraid to call anyone on what I believe is theft of my money, my life, or my future, any more. I refuse to feel guilty for things I had nothing to do with or tolerate those that think they can put it to me and I am not going to do anything about it. Guess again!

I will not tolerate a bad attitude when I am writing a check to you for service. If you can not be respectful and plaster a smile, either real or not on your face, since you are supposed to be working. I do not have to write the big check for poor service and I will just leave the items I was going to purchase, right in front of you and you can just put them back yourself.

If I cannot hear my music because yours is too loud, then I will let you know it and you had better respect that.

I will help educate those who will be educated.

I will respect those who respect me.

I do not want to see your rear end or underwear as you walk with your pants down around your knees, get a belt, this is not a fad, this is stupid and indecent.

I don't want to hear your phone conversation while I am trying to eat, shop or wait to be served, use your cell phone away from people you don't know, and I will do the same.

I will not be coerced into taking smaller and drier pieces of chicken, because I am white and you are black and you are sticking it to "whitey". I will call you on it, and request a manager. This happened to us the last time at the Popeye's in Valdosta, Georgia. We had noticed it a couple of other times, but this one was obvious!

I am not going to allow those sent to represent me, give my money away without me being ok with it.

I want accountability for each and every dime, and if it is an assistance program, it will have a limit to how much and for how long. No more Mr. Nice Guy!

If you let a criminal out of jail by mistake or some change of heart, you will be held personally accountable if they go out and repeat the offense.

If you go to jail, no more cushy cells, you will work off your time and that does not mean getting educated on my dime, or bulking up so you can really do damage, and if you are proven to have molested anyone, no second chances!

I like Bill O'reilly's "Jessica's Law – 1st offense you get 25 years! If every state does not adopt this law, then there is something very wrong within those states constituency.

If you are going to have your body tattooed and pierced all over, fine, I just don't want to see it. I don't go around showing you my cellulite...

Fads are fine – within reason, belt your pants, and I don't want to know how well endowed you may or may not be!

If I call you and leave a message, return the call, because if you don't I will go to the next level until I get resolve. I called because there is an issue, not because I wanted to push 10,000 numbers to get to your voicemail.

If you are a company who hides behind voice mail, then I will try my level best not to do business with you, and I will spread the word. Let's see, how much does it cost today to replace a customer – let's just say, a lot more than you can afford if you lose a bunch a day. If I am calling, I need help.

If you have more kids than you can support, I am not going to feel sorry for you and I am not going to give you one red cent!

If you have a hankering to be on alcohol or drugs, I am not going to help you, we all have choices, so you had better find a way back yourself. This world is for the strong, not the weak, so if you cannot handle life – go to another country where they will take care of your sorry ass.

I am not going to cover you when you can not work because you partied too much last nite, or have some other more important thing to do other than work, so now I have to cover for you! I don't think so.

I don't want to hear, "ok I will AX someone". Unless, you are planning on using a cutting device on someone, I expect you to pronounce the word ASK and if you don't, I will correct you, because I am trying to help you. Try this simple test. Say Task, Flask, Mask, ok, now ask! By George you got it!

I recently had occasion when seeking help via the telephone with Wachovia Bank. The so called Customer Service person answering the phone was rude, had an attitude and did not seem to understand that she was there to HELP. After getting nowhere with her, I asked for the supervisor, she said she would "ax the supervisor if she could talk to me", at which time I replied, "ok then ax her". She immediately shot back, "what did you say", and I repeated it, "ok go AX her". She was ticked, she knew exactly what I was saying to her and why and she did not like it. She could speak quite well otherwise and there was no reason for an inappropriate word such as that. You know what I am talking about. You will hear it from some folks, even on TV, even those supposedly educated. NO one corrects them. Why not? There are so many good role models out there, listen to them, model yourself after them, not those who feel they have to be different. If you are going to be different, have some great talent that sets you apart. Don't speak incorrectly, dress like a clown, walk like you have some crippling problem, or have more colors than a paint pallet painted forever on any exposed skin surface, or drive down the street pounding bass that gives me a headache in less than 3 seconds.

I know that becoming responsible and accountable comes with a price of doing the right thing, doing the best you can, working hard, believing and supporting your country, believing that if you can help someone to achieve a higher level in life, you should do it.

When I returned to the work force after raising my son, it was a rude awakening. I found that glass ceiling you hear about. I was not deterred though.

I was 38 and I felt like I had a whole world to discover again. I got a great job, and in a few weeks, it became apparent that the company I loved so, had not been run so well. It was in dire financial straits, I did not know it, but I found out quickly, I along with about 150 others got our lay off notices one Friday. Now I tell you I did not want to leave that job, it was my new beginning, my new future. I was in a state of shock, but as I was leaving, my boss stuck several pieces of paper in my hand and told me to call any of these people, they knew about me and wanted to talk to me, and it would be ok. Please note I did not run to my local unemployment office or apply for every "entitlement known to man"! I wanted to work!

Well, I drove home with tears streaming down my face, thinking this could not be happening to me. I had never lost a job, even if it was not my fault, but I did the first thing, that I could, I opened up the pieces of paper, laid them out alphabetically and saw the names and numbers. I called the one beginning with A. A wonderful lady answered and once she found out my name, said how soon can you come in to chat, I told her Monday, and at 9:30 a.m. on Monday, I was offered a job.

It was a position I had never had before, but I knew I could learn whatever they would be willing to teach me. I started the next day, and 6 years later, and after many promotions and going back and getting my college degree, I am so glad I called. I am so glad that, in those few weeks, when I started back to work, I worked as hard as I did, because I was noticed and people were willing to open doors for me, even when their doors were closing too.

I often remember that boss who took the time to make some phone calls for me because he saw willingness and eagerness, and I hope that he faired as well as I did, I am sure he did, people who care enough to help those who are trying so hard, have to be rewarded too.

I have had a great life, not perfect, not easy, and when the chips were down, I got a second job to get me through the bad times. A single mom may have a few more obstacles, but if she is trying, help her. Not because she is a woman, not because she is not aided by a spouse bringing home another check, but because she is trying. Give her every opportunity to learn, grow, and spread her wings to success. Give her the promotion because she deserves it, not because you need a woman in that spot. Some of the most wonderful, successful women I have known, started out exactly that way, and through perseverance and hard work, made it. They are heroes to me. One of them had 4 daughters she raised, she got her degree along the way and became an Executive Vice President of a very well known company.

When I started back to work, she spent time after hours helping me learn as quickly as I could, the new job she had hired me to do, even though I had no prior experience. I asked her why, she responded "You have the ability to be a Star, and I want to help that process begin". I don't know if I reached stardom, but I did well, and it was directly attributable to her and a few others along the way.

We all know star potential people, we just need to take the time to let them know we are aware of that potential and we just want to help them on their way. Young and old, male and female, they are all around us. Watch for them, take the time to correct them for their betterment, lead by example, and be patient. It will pay dividends to us all.

Help America stand up, by helping those coming after us to carry the torch to success and keep our great country shining bright into the darkness of tomorrow.

CHAPTER 14
I DON'T REMEMBER INVITING YOU

Appears that we're slow learners....Theodore Roosevelt on Immigrants and being an AMERICAN

"In the first place we should insist that if the immigrant who comes here in good faith becomes an American and assimilates himself to us, he shall be treated on an exact equality with everyone else, for it is an outrage to discriminate against any such man because of creed, or birthplace, or origin. But this is predicated upon the man's becoming in very fact an American, and nothing but an American... There can be no divided allegiance here. Any man who says he is an American, but something else also, isn't an American at all. We have room for but one flag, the American flag, and this excludes the red flag, which symbolizes all wars against liberty and civilization, just as much as it excludes any foreign flag of a nation to which we are hostile...We have room for but one language here, and that is the English language...and we have room for but one sole loyalty and that is a loyalty to the American people."

Theodore Roosevelt 1907

I don't go to your country and try to make you change to make me happier and more comfortable, so don't do it to me.

Why is everyone coming here? Clue, they like the freedom!

Now mine is in jeopardy because of all of these strangers coming here and trying to make it like the place they left.

Here are my thoughts, IF YOU LOVED IT SO MUCH THERE AND YOU MISS WHAT YOU HAD THERE - GO HOME!

We moved South for the sun and fun and an easier lifestyle! We did not want to change anything and make it like Washington, DC. in fact the farthest north we plan on ever going is Myrtle Beach, SC, we moved to the south for the change!

This must be rare though, because the majority of northerners coming south immediately want things to look like, feel like and be like what they left.

They take their big bucks from selling their homes up north, buy a bigger house for less money in the south, and brought an enormous attitude and think they are somebody really important. They start demanding grocery stores carry their favorite things they had up North, they must not trust the good ole southern neighbors, because they have to have bars and burglary alarms on their homes.

They push and shove themselves into everything. Fellow Americans are bad enough, but then the rest of the world has decided to move in and demand change. Well, my question to you too is – if you miss what you had up there – why don't you go back to where you came from.

I am tired of having to deal with Spanish, Russian, and any one of many Asian languages plus openly having to deal with your rituals and customs when I am out in my country. I promise I won't break into a couple of verses of Amazing Grace, if you will put out your incense in the nail parlor, I am the paying person! My country! Remember!

Well, it is true for those coming into our country. When I traveled abroad, I did my best to speak their language; no one started speaking English just to make it easier for me. Not even! So how come now we have to have everything in Spanish, and whatever else is the language of the day.

Sorry folks, learn our language or leave. I hate going to get a pedicure and listen to the foreign dialect being bantered around. I don't know if you are making fun of my feet or what, when you talk to each other and giggle and carry on! Unfortunately, you are the only game in town!

Simple. We have spent billions on changing everything here to make it easy on those, many of whom, have crept into our country. Wrong!!!

I need some help here. We need to take back our country. That does not mean not to have our children learn a foreign language, they need to expand their abilities, but that does not mean we have to have messages in 20 different languages, hey, I would just like to talk to a real person, if companies did not spend all of that money on messages in so many languages, they might actually be able to spend it on hiring capable people to take our calls and help us, which is why we are calling in the first place.

Oh yes, I am tired of having to deal with people I can not understand on the phone, or at the bank, or at the store. Someone who just looks at your blindly because they still speak any language but English, and this is who I need to ask for help. I don't think so. If a company can only hire this, I am not going there any more. I will not be spending my hard earned dollars for that and neither should you.

Story in Tampa Newspaper —Will we still be the Country of choice and still be America if we continue to make the changes forced on us by the people from other countries that came to live in America because it is the Country of Choice?

Think about it.

All I have to say is, when will they do something about MY RIGHTS? I celebrate Christmas, but because it isn't celebrated by everyone, we can no longer say Merry Christmas. Now it has to be Season's Greetings. It's not Christmas vacation, it's Winter Break. Isn't it amazing how this winter break ALWAYS occurs over the Christmas holiday? We've gone so far the other way, bent over backwards to not offend anyone, that I am now being offended. But it seems that no one has a problem with that.

This says it all!

This is an editorial written by an American citizen, published in a Tampa newspaper He did quite a job; didn't he? Read on, please!

IMMIGRANTS, NOT AMERICANS, MUST ADAPT.

I am tired of this nation worrying about whether we are offending some individual or their culture. Since the terrorist attacks on Sept. 11, we have experienced a surge in patriotism by the majority of Americans. However, the dust from the attacks had barely settled when the "politically correct! "crowd began complaining about the possibility that our patriotism was offending others.

I am not against immigration, nor do I hold a grudge against anyone who is seeking a better life by coming to America. Our population is almost entirely made up of descendants of immigrants. However, there are a few things that those who have recently come to our country, and apparently some born here, need to understand. This idea of America being a multicultural community has served only to dilute our sovereignty and our national identity. As Americans, we have our own culture, our own society, our own language and our own lifestyle. This culture has been developed over centuries of struggles, trials, and victories by millions of men and women who have sought freedom.

We speak ENGLISH, not Spanish, Portuguese, Arabic, Chinese, Japanese, Russian, or any other language.

Therefore, if you wish to become part of our society, learn the language!

"In God We Trust" is our national motto. This is not some Christian, right wing, and political slogan. We adopted this motto because Christian men and women, on Christian principles, founded this nation, and this is clearly documented. It is certainly appropriate to display it on the walls of our schools. If God offends you, then I suggest you consider another part of the world as your new home, because God is part of our culture.

If Stars and Stripes offend you, or you don't like Uncle Sam, then you should seriously consider a move to another part of this planet. We are happy with our culture and have no desire to change, and we really don't care how you did things where you came from. This is OUR COUNTRY, our land, and our lifestyle. Our First Amendment gives every citizen the right to express his opinion and we will allow you every opportunity! to do so. But once you are done complaining, whining, and griping about our flag, our pledge, our national motto, or our way of life, I highly encourage you take advantage of one other great American freedom, THE RIGHT TO LEAVE. AMEN

CHAPTER 15
I'M MAD, AS HELL AND
I AM NOT TAKING IT ANYMORE!

So just remember, if I see you in Wal-mart and you or your children throw things on the floor because you or they were too lazy to put it back on the shelf, I am going to pick it up and come after you to show you where it belongs, I am not afraid to do that any more.

I will donate to those who look like they are trying to get a life on line after this and any other disaster, but I am not giving you, who only take and have no respect for anything, one red cent. I don't have to!

Okay, now you politicians who make a living on begging for the black, Spanish, Asian and any other minority vote by giving away our country, I have news for you. You will not win anymore!

We need to make it possible that people like Ted, who needs to waddle off into the sunset, or go pray for forgiveness for his pathetic life, or Nancy, who I don't think set up a shelter in her district for these poor sad human beings after the hurricanes, and Harry, you need to fall on your knees today and start repenting for how you sold people up the river for your own personal gain.

The American people, of all political views, see or will be seeing you for what you are, only out for yourselves, padding your own bank accounts and letting the rest of us carry the payload. You see, I am not afraid to call you on it, and there will be more than just me in the not too distant future.

Where can we all begin? We have to identify the shortcomings. We have to identify ways to fix the past shortcomings and build toward a country that is truly unified and have a common purpose. Be all we can be. A country united cannot lose.

We have wealth, we have intelligence, we have loving hearts, and we have an abundance of talent given to us by a supreme being. No matter what our belief, our color, our heritage, our knowledge level, our degree of commitment, the common goal has to be to give what we have to make things better, not to be a taker, but to be an honorable, committed citizen.

We would not need so many prisons, if everyone knew that if you do something wrong, and everyone knew what was deemed to be wrong, you will pay a price back to your fellow citizens and country. The price is pretty much outlined by our laws, no interpretation needed by liberal judges. We rule by laws, we don't have people to put their interpretations on them, just like the Bible, the rules of right and wrong are obvious.

If a citizen of our country, hurts, by rape, murder or any other means, yes they are allowed a fair trial, but they will not use our monetary systems as a free ride until they can find an attorney to find a loophole to get them off. Limitations and no cushy jail cell, jail is not a vacation, it is a penalty for doing wrong.

Welfare will go away. Any able bodied individual will be forced to find a job, If there are reasons why not, then there are programs to put them in that can take care of serving the public and getting paid a fair sum for it. No free checks. No free housing, no subsidies for able-bodied persons. Any subsidies, to the elderly or children will be tightly monitored for everyone's sake. No one has a clue how much is given away either through fraud, or collusion. It can be done.

When our children go to school, they will be taught that hats come off, clothes fit, respect for the teachers, respect for property. They will all learn to speak without sounding like they have a mouth full of mush. We know everyone, unless they have a speech impediment, can speak correctly and distinctly. We don't need Ebonics, or rap; it serves no purpose in our society. There is no need to be different by wearing obscene clothes, or walking any other way that straight, and tall. NO slumping, no shucking and jiving, no gangs allowed, we won't need weapon checks as our kids try to get to class!

We all have space, respect it.

If you want something I have, then get a job and save up for it, because that is what I have done. We all have the same opportunities, we just have to know what they are and go for it.

I am not going to not get a job promotion for a job that I can do better than any one else, because you do not have a certain number of a color. Wrong, wrong.

Equality is what America is built on. Let us put it back on track.

Wherever you live, take care it. Pick up the trash so it does not blow into my space, I will do the same. If you don't you will be fined for it. Keep your home maintained, if you cannot do it; apply for a loan to get it done. Believe me if everyone is working that can work, and if they are moving up in their career, no matter what it is, because they deserve to and want to. You will have the funds to take care of your home and family. I am not going to do it for you. If you do not, and won't do it, then you do not deserve to have it.

CHAPTER 16
NO MORE LIES

My generation grew up believing in truth, that the news was truthfully told, the pictures we saw were not doctored. That is not longer true. How can we expect our citizenry to be honorable when we see our Federal officials setting each other up, lying and false advertising. Do not accept it, I will not. We have the power to turn them off. If you choose to believe it, then I don't want to be around you, and I won't be. Honor is honor.

Teach it to your children, live it in your life.

We have power! Power to turn off a channel that is showing things our children do not need to be exposed to. We have power to turn the channel, not buy a newspaper, magazine or not attend a concert that is contrast to honor and good. It will go away if it is not listened too. You have power. Use it! Use it for Good though.

I watch our children as parents, and I have to say, I smile with pride, because much to their children's unhappiness sometimes, they don't give up or give in. It has to be tough today, but I know these two sets of parents are producing what will be 7 contributing, hardworking, and respectful American citizens. I will bet on this, and I am not a betting woman!

They cut the kids no slack, they reward success and obedience and no long hair, goofy clothes, bad grades or lying is acceptable. The kids are well rounded, involved in sports and trying hard to do the right thing, and I hear yes ma'am and no ma'am, and yes sir, no sir, even to their parents. Both sets of parents work together as a team on the raising of the children. All 4 parents work too, keep nice clean homes, do not allow the kids to watch the wrong things on TV or play video games that are not good for them. They know what is going on in their kids' lives at home and at school. How cool is that? Is this unusual? It shouldn't be, but I think it must be.

All you read about is kids getting into trouble, no body home, flunking out of school or not even going. Our children work hard, long hours and are tired, but they always find time for the children and to stay involved. Not easy, not even, but they do. It takes effort and it starts at home and it starts early.

Is it worth it? From where I sit watching these young people grow into good, courteous, clean respectful adults, you bet.

We are letting other people rule our minds, and we don't have too. If we do right, if we pave our own way, if we try to do the right thing, and expect the same from those around us, times won't change, people will, and all for the better.

CHAPTER 17
WHAT CAN WE DO

I end with this:

"The greatest good you can do for another is not to share your riches, but to reveal to him his own". – Benjamin Disraeli

How wonderful are those words, how powerful are those words?

Please let us not forget that so many have gone before us dying for our great Country, we cannot have let that be in vain. If I have stepped on some toes, I am not going to apologize. I have a right too!

I beg you help me get our Country up where it once was. Straight, tall and proud. We can do it. I don't think there are many who are not willing to help anyone who will carry his or her weight. You just have to try and it takes the masses.

Do your best and you will have a pay check, you will have a home to take care of, you will have children who come home at night and you don't have to go and see behind bars on "visitation" days.

If you see someone you can help along the way, do it, you will be so glad you did. Pray for each other, everyday, not just when you need something.

There are good and bad days for us all. There are honest people we can put into office to represent us. We must find them and make sure we hold them accountable for their actions and decisions.

We all have the same breaks. For those among us who are ill or lacking in some way or need a helping hand, we will, with our God's help, whoever that God is in your heart, carry us all forward.

It takes all, Republican, Democrat, Independent, it does not matter, this is our country, and if we disagree on some things, we believe in one thing together – we love our country and we just want people to be accountable for their actions. You, me, our children, our grand-children, it has to be this way, or we will not be able to get our U. S. A. up again. Lady Liberty cannot carry that torch alone, it takes us all with the grace of God and faith.

We decide who represents us, we decide how hard we want to work, we decide how we live our lives, and we deserve honesty, respect and an equal opportunity. If you deserve these things, then you have to give them back to others.

God Bless America and our land of freedom, please help us to get control again and leave our children and grandchildren a better place, they deserve that. This can be our legacy and it can be a great one.

A father wanted to read a magazine but was being bothered by his little girl, Shelby. She wanted to know what the United States looked like. Finally, he tore a sheet out of his new magazine on which was printed the map of the country. Tearing it into small pieces, he gave it to Shelby, and said, "Go into the other room and see if you can put this together. This will show you our whole country today."

After a few minutes, Shelby returned and handed him the map correctly fitted together. The father was surprised and asked how she had finished so quickly.

"Oh," she said, "on the other side of the paper is a picture of Jesus. When I got all of Jesus back where He belonged, then our country just came together."

One Nation under GOD, and in GOD we trust! Don't let people who think they can take this away from us, succeed!

End Notes

See TANF Financial Data for years 1997 to 2004 - Appendix A

See 2004 TANF Federal Funds spent breakdown by state – Appendix B

See TANF Financial Combined Federal Funds spent in FY2004 – Appendix C

See TANF State breakdowns by state

About the Author

Judy Forster is a wife, mother and grandmother and resides happily with her husband in a quiet community in southeastern Georgia.

Judy was born in Los Angeles, California, spent her teenage years in southern Indiana and moved to the Washington, DC metropolitan area in 1973. At age 38, after being a stay at home Mom for twelve years, she went back to college. She received her BS degree in Business Administration and re-entered the work force and enjoyed a great career in banking and real estate.

Judy wrote this book after witnessing the mayhem following Hurricane Katrina. To her it was proof positive, that people don't and won't take responsibility for their actions and choices, from the people who could have left but didn't, to the government officials placed in jobs to manage the process after the storm, pointing fingers at everyone else for not doing their job.

The cameras focused on the thousands demanding everything and blaming everyone, and the government officials agreeing with them and mandating that WE had to make it go away.

You may not agree with all of this book or Judy's personal opinions, but, ponder the many facts that support the out of control situation of our country. Judy's endeavor is to help lead to change. To solicit everyone to help get our youth back on track, to rid the U.S. of the "give me" attitude and raise the disadvantaged to levels of responsibility and achievement.

Her faith in God, her willingness to work hard, her belief that teaching responsibility and accountability will lead to success has been her motivation and she needs your help.

Watch for Judy's next book on the missing customer service in America.

www.ingramcontent.com/pod-product-compliance
Lightning Source LLC
Chambersburg PA
CBHW020307290526
45784CB00003B/1404